Victorious Bible Curriculum

THE BEGINNING (PART 1 OF 9)

God created a home for mankind, and placed us in it to tend and guard it as His image. When we rebelled, God promised a seed of the woman to one day restore creation — and preserved that seed when our violence filled the world.

THE PATRIARCHS (PART 2 OF 9)

God chose Abraham to be the custodian of the line through which the promised redeemer would come. Abraham's grandson Jacob became the father of the twelve tribes of Israel, a nation that would bless the whole earth.

THE EXODUS (PART 3 OF 9)

For 400 years, God grew Jacob's tiny family into a nation. Through Moses, He released them from slavery to give them a new home. Despite the faithless first generation's rebellion, their children would inherit the promised land.

CONQUEST AND JUDGMENT (PART 4 OF 9)

Under Joshua, the children of the exodus conquered the promised land. After they settled in, they fell into idolatry and suffered under foreign domination. Time after time, they needed God's deliverance through a head-crushing judge.

THE KINGDOM OF ISRAEL (PART 5 OF 9)

God used Israel's first kings, the vacillating Saul and the head-crusher David, to give Israel peace. Solomon built a prosperous kingdom, which then split and fell into idolatry. After 70 years' exile in Babylon, God restored them to the land.

THE COMING OF THE MESSIAH (PART 6 OF 9)

The long wait for the serpent-crushing redeemer came to an end with the birth of Jesus of Nazareth. Raised in Galilee and baptized in the Jordan, He began to proclaim the kingdom of God and demonstrate God's love and power.

THE MINISTRY OF JESUS (PART 7 OF 9)

The blind could see, the sick were healed, the dead raised. The kingdom of God was truly at hand. But the leaders of Israel rejected the One God had sent to save them from their sins and deliver them into God's kingdom.

JESUS' FINAL DAYS (PART 8 OF 9)

On Thursday, before His arrest, Jesus ate one final meal with His disciples. Then He was arrested, beaten, falsely accused, tried, convicted and crucified. But death could not hold Him and the grave could not contain Him.

THE BEGINNING OF THE CHURCH (PART 9 OF 9)

After His resurrection, Jesus' followers received the power of the Holy Spirit to disciple the nations of the world, baptizing them and teaching them all that Jesus had said. Christ's body grew and began to crush the enemy's head under her foot.

Copyright © 2016 by Joe Anderson and Tim Nichols

All rights reserved
Printed in the United States of America
First Edition

No part of this book may be reproduced in any form or by any electronic or mechanical means, including information storage and retrieval systems, except for brief quotations in printed reviews, without the prior permission of the author.

Unless otherwise indicated, all Scripture quotations are taken from the New King James Version®. Copyright © 1982 by Thomas Nelson, Inc. Used by permission. All rights reserved.

Scripture quotations marked (NIV) are taken from the Holy Bible, New International Version®, NIV®. Copyright © 1973, 1978, 1984, 2011 by Biblica, Inc.™ Used by permission of Zondervan. All rights reserved worldwide. www.zondervan.com The "NIV" and "New International Version" are trademarks registered in the United States Patent and Trademark Office by Biblica, Inc.™

Author's translation or paraphrase indicated by an asterisk after the reference.

Illustrations by Gustave Doré
Colorized and modified by William Britton

Praise for Headwaters Bible Curriculum

These lessons are not just a way to teach the Bible to middle school kids. As I read the lessons, I found both my head and my heart irresistibly engaged. Joe and Tim have opened the grace and truth of God's Word in a way that seriously lifts us towards Christ while nudging us outward towards the world. I recommend these studies for both devotional and motivational reading!

Dave Cheadle, President of the Rocky Mountain Classis, Reformed Church of America

While I have spent quite a bit of time studying the Bible myself, I find your ideas and themes to be real food for thought and they help tie together much of the story God is telling throughout... I've already talked with people about your curriculum and have recommended they look into it for their own families. I can't loan out my copy for their perusal, because I'm using it everyday!

Linda Kidder, Home Educator, Colorado

I LOVE THIS BOOK!!!! We're just finishing up the Garden narrative. We've had such fruitful discussions—I have been pleased with it in every way. In fact, I'm hoping our church will start using it. I haven't had any problems or difficulties using the curriculum, I ONLY have good things to say about it. In fact, I'm in danger of writing in all caps I'm so enthusiastic about it.

Leah Robinson, Home Educator, Texas

I am really enjoying having this resource to work from and steer our lessons!

Christy Johnson, Bible Teacher, Bingham Academy, Ethiopia

Our family actually loves the curriculum. My children are in 5th and 8th grade and the content has suited both of their levels perfectly. To this point we hadn't found a curriculum that taught the Bible at such a detailed level that has also kept the kids engaged. We've had to slow down on the materials because otherwise they would be through them well before the school year is up. We are planning on buying the rest of the series.

Chris Turner, Home Educator, Colorado

How to Use This Book

This series of little manuals walks you through the biblical Story from end to end. Just read. Here are a few things you might want to keep in mind as you read through the Story.

- Try to love the characters. God does....
- The story is written in such a way as to make sin look stupid, but remember that the characters are all real people. No matter how stupid the choice, a real person actually looked at the options and then picked that particular one for reasons that seemed pretty good at the time. Nobody gets up in the morning and says, "I'm going to make stupid life choices that people will be mocking for centuries." Try to see it from their point of view. Ask yourself, "Why did this look like a good idea at the time?" That's how you learn to recognize temptations. It's easy to see sinful and stupid choices for what they are in hindsight, but in the moment it's often very hard. So learn to think through what these choices looked like from the inside, in the heat of the moment — you'll be amazed what you learn about yourself.
- Pay attention to the patterns. We'll point out a bunch of them as we go through the Story, but try to spot them yourself, too. If you can learn to read the Word and see the patterns in the Story, you will become able to read the world around you and see the patterns in the story God is telling right now.
- Each lesson comes with a psalm. The psalms provide us with another lens through which to look at the Story, and God has a lot to teach us that way. Sometimes we've given you an activity that will help integrate the psalm with that episode in the Story. Other times, we've just given you the psalm, and we're going to let you fill in the blanks. Read over the psalm a few times, then go into the lesson and see what comes to you. You'll be surprised what you can learn.
- As with any book that talks about Scripture, don't necessarily take our word for anything. Imagine you're sitting in a living room or around a campfire with us, and we're just talking about the Story. You're free to disagree, correct, challenge our understanding. The Word is the authority, not us — so grab your Bible and look things up yourself.

You'll find a section labeled "Activities" following the lesson. The point of this section is to immerse you as deeply in the Story as possible, through prayer, meditation on the Story, and other exercises. The "Evaluation" questions at the end of each lesson will help you to check your understanding of the material.

For Small Group Leaders
Have everyone in the group read the lesson ahead of time. Depending on how involved your group is, you can have them engage some or all of the activities, or you can save those for group time when you're together. The evaluation questions might serve as discussion starters if the conversation lags.

For Homeschoolers
Have your student read the lesson and complete the activities. (Some might be more appropriate as whole-family activities.) You can use the evaluation questions as a quiz or as discussion starters to check your student's comprehension of the lesson.

Table of Contents

Unit 3 Abraham, Isaac and Jacob 7
    Lesson 3.1 God's Answer to the Fall, Flood and Babel: God Called and Divided Abram 9
    Lesson 3.2 God Created a Seed-Nation with a Covenant 17
    Lesson 3.3 God Fulfilled His Promise: The Seed-Son Born and Protected from Two Threats 23
    Lesson 3.4 God Tested and Evaluated Abraham 29
    Lesson 3.5 Isaac and Rebekah: The Chosen Son Married and Came of Age 35
    Lesson 3.6 Jacob, Esau, and the Birthright 43
    Lesson 3.7 Jacob Prepared in Exile 49

Unit 4 Jacob's Family 59
    Lesson 4.1 Jacob's Family in the Land 61
    Lesson 4.2 Joseph's Dreams and Betrayal by His Brothers 69
    Lesson 4.3 Joseph and Judah Came of Age in Foreign Lands 77
    Lesson 4.4 Joseph's Brothers Tested in Egypt 87
    Lesson 4.5 Joseph Restored to His Family 95

UNIT 3: THE PATRIARCHS

In response to humanity's threefold fall, God would create a nation that would be the custodian of His revelation and the seed-line, but He started with one childless man, Abram. God called (commanded) Abram to leave his country and his family connections behind and go to a land God would show him. God promised that He would make Abram a great nation that would bless the whole world. Abram obeyed, dividing himself from his family to sojourn in the land, prefiguring Israel's history by going to Egypt when there was a famine in the land of Canaan. God brought plagues on Pharaoh, and Abram returned to Canaan. When he returned to the land, Abram divided from Lot and planted roots until the land was attacked; then Abram went on a conquest in the land. After the battle, Abram was blessed by Melchizedek and found rest—but he was still childless.

God promised Abram a son, but the seed-line was continually under threat. Abram's faith faltered, and he stepped outside his marriage to bear a son with Hagar; but God restored him and reaffirmed the promise of a son, changing his name from Abram to Abraham. Abraham tried to protect his family by lying about his relationship with Sarah, but God made sure he got caught in the lies, and still protected him better than he could have protected himself. After Isaac was born, Ishmael posed a different sort of threat, but God protected Isaac's inheritance, while also protecting Ishmael and Hagar.

God tested Abraham by commanding him to go to Mt. Moriah to offer his promised son Isaac as an ascension offering. Believing that God would raise Isaac from the dead, Abraham obeyed, but God stopped him at the last second and provided a substitute lamb. God then evaluated Abraham and rewarded him for his obedience with promises of descendants and an inheritance.

Isaac married and started a family, and God blessed him and made him great so that he had peace with his brother and his neighbors, but there was trouble within his house. God had promised Isaac's son Jacob the ruling blessing, but Isaac favored his son Esau. Rebekah arranged for Jacob to get the blessing anyway; but Jacob had to flee to his uncle Laban so Esau would not kill him. On the way to his uncle's house, God met Jacob and promised to bless him and make him great. Although he entered Laban's house a poor refugee and Laban constantly tried to cheat him, God's word came to pass, and He brought Jacob out of Laban's house with a large family and great wealth.

LESSON 3.1

God's Answer to the Fall, Flood and Babel: God Called and Divided Abram

UNIT 3

THE STORY

Lesson Theme - Abram's call followed Genesis' pattern and prefigured Israel's history.

Up to this point in the Story, there have been three "falls." Adam and Eve fell when they ate from the tree of the knowledge of good and evil. God responded by kicking them out of the garden and cursing creation. Then the whole earth grew up modeling the wickedness of Cain. God responded by flooding the earth and starting over with Noah's family. Finally, Noah's descendants built their own city to make themselves into their own gods. God responded by confusing their languages and scattering them to the ends of the earth. Three falls, three acts of God's discipline, and still no solution to the problems that Adam and Eve had brought into the world through their disobedience. Of course, this was not because God was stumbling around trying to figure out what to do; rather, God was permitting the fall to work its way out into the corners of humanity before He began the process of redeeming all humanity and all creation.

In this lesson, we see the beginning of God's answer to this threefold fall and the beginning of His ultimate redemption. God was using Abram to create a seed-nation, and Abram's life followed the fourfold pattern of God's creative activity (command, divide, name and evaluate). In this lesson, we see that God created the seed-nation when He **commanded** Abram to go to the land He would show him and **divided** Abram from his family.

OVERVIEW

In this lesson, we see God's answer to the threefold fall of humanity: God called (commanded) Abram out of his country to go to the land that He would show him, and God promised Abram blessings as He guided his future. Abram obeyed and found himself in the land of Canaan, divided from his family and his homeland. God was creating a seed-nation, and as the patriarch of Israel, Abram prefigured Israel's later history. He went to Egypt when there was a famine in the land of Canaan; God brought plagues on Pharaoh, and Abram returned to Canaan. When he returned to the land, Abram divided from Lot and planted roots until the land was attacked; then Abram went on a conquest in the land. After the battle, Abram was blessed by Melchizedek and found rest.

SOURCE MATERIAL

- Genesis 11:27-14:24
- Hebrews 11:8-10
- Psalm 59
- Proverbs 13:20

Abram's call and God's fourfold creation process
In the creation narrative, we introduced you to the fourfold process by which God created the heavens and the earth. On each day, God commanded something into existence, divided that which was newly created, named the divided parts and then evaluated His creation. In this

9

Unit 3: Abraham, Isaac and Jacob

OBJECTIVES

Feel...

- impressed by Abram's commitment to step out in faith.
- awe that Noah's curse on Canaan (and blessing on Shem and Japheth) was being fulfilled 300 years after he spoke it.
- impressed by Abram's willingness to give back all the spoils of Sodom in order to be sure that God would receive the glory for his wealth.

Understand...

- the first hints of correspondence between Abram's life and Israel's history.
- the promises made to Abram and how he obeyed God in faith.
- the outworking of Noah's curse on Canaan in the enslavement of his descendants by a Shemite king.
- Lot's mistake in moving close to and eventually into Sodom.
- that Melchizedek's presence indicated that, although it was uncommon to worship Yahweh during Abram's time, not everyone had forsaken Him.

Apply this understanding by...

- considering what things God might be calling you to.
- taking concrete steps to obey God's calling on your life.
- anticipating God's blessing upon your life from unexpected people, just as Melchizedek blessed Abram.

lesson, God is in the beginning stages of creating His chosen people. He **commanded** Abram to leave his country, and He **divided** him from his people (Gen 12:1). Later, God would give Abram a new name and evaluate him (we'll see these in future lessons). So Abram's life maps onto the creation pattern as shown below:

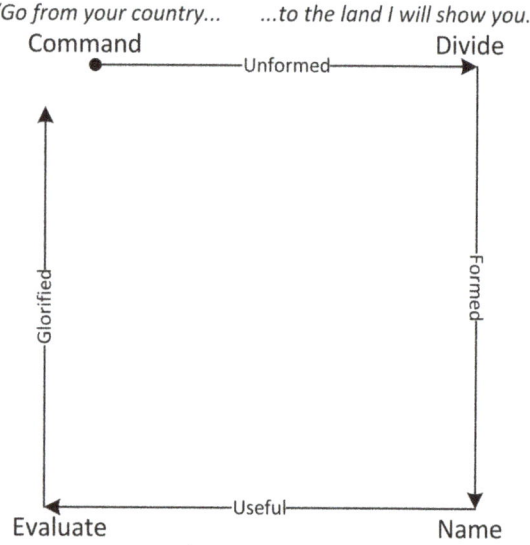

Figure 3.1a *God commands and divides Abram*

The command given to Abram was accompanied by seven promises (Gen 12:2-3). These promises were the foundation of God's covenant with Abram which would establish the terms of God's relationship to Israel and the world. Refer to the outline for the seven promises. Watch for these to be fulfilled in the life of Abram and his sons and later with the nation of Israel.

Abram obeyed God without questioning Him. When he got to the land, God visited him and told him that this was the land he was going to receive (Gen 12:7). Everywhere Abram went, he built an altar to the Lord. He built one in response to God's promise, then he moved to a place between Bethel and Ai where he built another altar (Gen 12:8). There was not yet a central place of worship, and so Abram functioned as a traveling priest, building places of worship everywhere he went.

Abram's life prefigured Israel's later history
A series of events happened in Abram's life that were later paralleled by the nation of Israel. The basic fourfold pattern of Israel's history is childhood, training, conquest and rest. We will see each of these in the life of Abram.

The events in Genesis 12:10-20 correspond to the **childhood** (bondage in Egypt) period of Israel's history. Notice the similarities between Abram's life and Israel: there was a famine in the land of Canaan (as in Jacob's day); Abram and his family went to Egypt to get food (like Jacob's family would later do); Abram's wife was taken into Pharaoh's household (like Israel would later become slaves to Pharaoh); God brought plagues on Pharaoh, and Abram was sent back to Canaan with spoil (like Israel was during the exodus).

Following his return to Canaan, Abram went to the place where he had built the altar between Bethel and Ai (Gen 13:3-4). Abram then separated from Lot. Lot chose the fertile land to the east of the Jordan, while Abram dwelt in the arid hill country of southern Judea. This was a period of testing **(training)** for Abram; he wandered in the land, but it wasn't a land of milk and honey. Nevertheless, God promised that the land of Canaan was his inheritance; in response to God's presence, Abram built another altar to the Lord (Gen 13:18).

Abram's **conquest** in Genesis 14 corresponds to Joshua's conquest of the land of Canaan (which followed Israel's exodus, just as it followed Abram's exodus). Chedorlaomer was a Shemite who was allied with four other kings. They were ruling over the Canaanites and extorting tribute taxes from them. For 12 years, the Canaanites faithfully payed their taxes, but in the 13th year they decided to rebel (Gen 14:4). Notice here that the Canaanites were serving a Shemite (remember Noah's prophecy—Gen 9:25-27).

In response to their rebellion, Chedorlaomer's alliance made battle against the land of the Canaanites and defeated them from north to south. When they got down to the valley of Siddim (where the Dead Sea is now), the kings of Sodom and Gomorrah as well as several other Canaanite kings made battle against Chedorlaomer's alliance. Chedorloamer won and captured Lot in the process (Gen 14:12).

Abram was allied with several other Canaanites, and together (under Abram's leadership) they chased down Chedorlaomer's alliance and defeated them (Gen 14:15). They chased them as far as Dan in the north of Israel, saved the possessions of Sodom and Gomorrah, and rescued Lot. Having defeated Chedorlaomer's alliance,

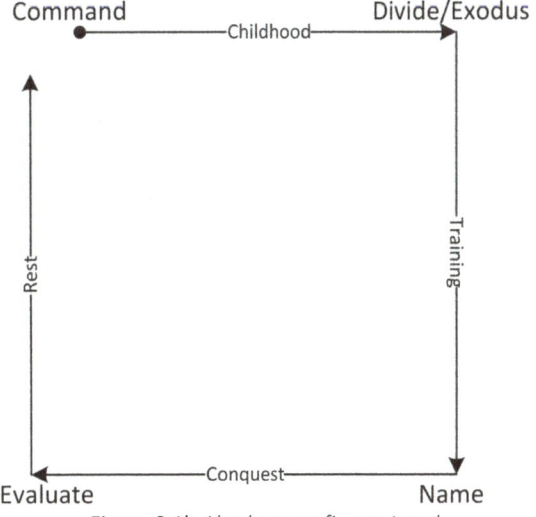

Figure 3.1b *Abraham prefigures Israel*

Abram replaced Chedorlaomer and became the de-facto ruler of the land of Canaan. (As a side note, Abram was a descendant of Eber who was a son of Arphaxad, the younger brother of Elam of whom Chedorlaomer was a descendant; we see here that the younger son was replacing the elder.) Of course, Abram didn't take control of the land at this time, for it was not yet his time.

Following his conquest of the land, Abram entered the **rest**. Rest is associated with bread and wine throughout the Bible; here Melchizedek brought Abram bread and wine and blessed him (Gen 14:18-19). Abram engaged in another Sabbath activity by giving God a tithe of all that he had.

Notice that Melchizedek was the first person whom Abram met who also worshiped Yahweh. This would have been an unexpected encouragement for Abram; when you set out to follow God's direction for your life, He puts unexpected people in your way who will encourage you.

APPLICATION

God commanded Abram to leave his country and his people to go to a land that God would show to him. Throughout this curriculum, you will have chances to work their way around the diagram above (Figure 3.1a). For now, start thinking about what God has called you to and some concrete steps you can take in that direction. At this point in your life, your calling might be as simple as "obey your parents" or "learn to pray." Abram didn't know where he would end up or the adventures he would enjoy along the way, but nevertheless, he put one foot in front of the other and went where God told him to go.

ACTIVITIES

1. The Promises Fulfilled. God made seven promises to Abram in Genesis 12:1-3. List those promises below. Then read through Genesis 12-14:24 and look for places where those promises were fulfilled in one way or another. Of course, none of the promises were fully filled right away, but these are the kind of promises that can be fulfilled many times and in many ways. Put a check mark by each promise that you see fulfilled in Genesis 12-14:24. _____

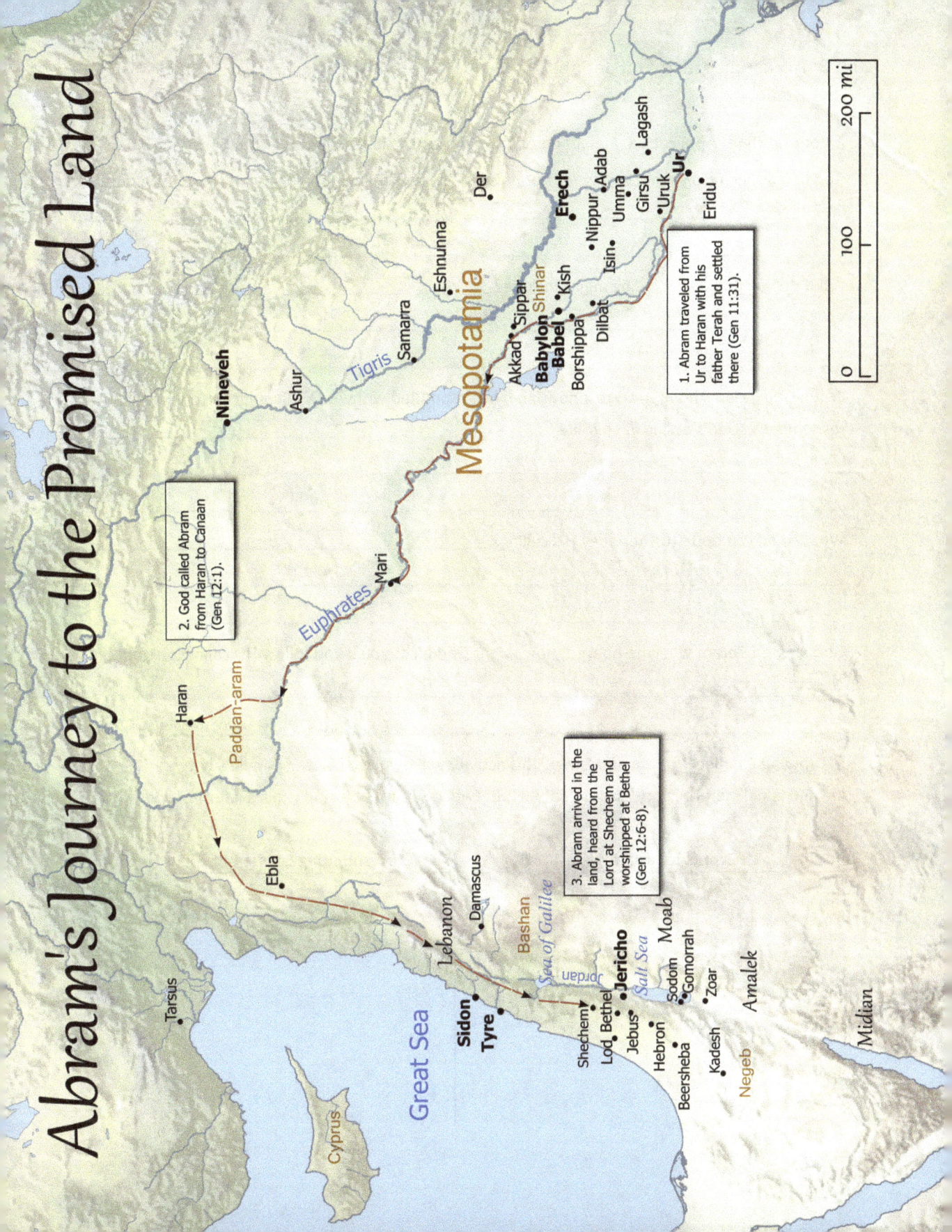

Unit 3: Abraham, Isaac and Jacob

2. Journal Time: Application. Reflect on Abram's life and calling and answer the questions below. God had a specific plan and calling for Abram's life. Do you believe God has a specific calling for your life? _____

_____

What do you think your calling might include?_____

_____

_____

When God called Abram to go to a new land, he responded with quick obedience. How have you responded to God's calling in your life?_____

_____

_____

What could you do to further obey His calling?_____

_____

_____

God blessed Abram when he obeyed; how might God bless you if you follow His calling on your life?___

_____

_____

3. Drawing Parallels: Abram and Israel. This activity will help you see the parallels between Abram's life and Israel's later history. List the parallels between Abram's life and Israel's later history.

Events in Abram's Life	Corresponding Events of Israel's History

Lesson 3.1

EVALUATION

1. In what ways did Abram's call parallel God's fourfold creative activity? _____
_____
_____
_____

2. How many promises were made to Abram when God called him out of his homeland? _____
   Name three of these. _____
_____
_____
_____

3. What was Lot's mistake? _____
_____
_____

   What happened to Lot as a result? _____
_____
_____

4. Who was Melchizedek? _____
_____
_____

   What did he do for Abram? _____
_____
_____

   How do you suppose this made Abram feel? _____
_____
_____
_____

LESSON 3.2

God Created a Seed-Nation with a Covenant: God Named Abraham and Promised Him a Son

UNIT 3

THE STORY

Lesson Theme - God's faithfulness to Abram even when he failed

In spite of God's clear promise that he and his wife would have a son, Abram took matters into his own hands and slept with Sarai's servant Hagar. In spite of Abram's sin, God did not renege on His promise. Instead, He reaffirmed His promise, gave Abram a new name and continued to make Abram's life useful. God is faithful even when we are faithless. Nevertheless, Abram's actions had tangible consequences in the real world.

God's covenant with Abram

God had promised that Abram would become a great nation (Gen 12:2-3), but in order to become a nation, he would need to have a lot of descendants, and in order to have descendants, he would need to have a son...one son at the very least. By Genesis 15, Abram was old enough to know that if he hadn't had kids yet, he wasn't going to. In order to assure Abram that he would indeed have a son, God appeared to him to reaffirm His promise.

The first thing Abram spoke to the Lord in this interaction amounted to, "Hey, what happened to that son You promised? Should I make my servant my heir?" (Gen 15:2-3). God assured Abram that he would indeed have a son from his own body and that son would be his heir. In fact, God told Abram that his descendants would be as numerous as the stars in the sky (Gen 15:4-5).

OVERVIEW

God established His covenant with Abram, confirming his name, "great father," by promising him a son. But Abram's faith faltered, and he stepped outside his marriage to bear a son with Hagar, thus falling from his calling. God restored him, however, named him, and continued to use him to establish the seed-line.

SOURCE MATERIAL

- Genesis 15-19
- Psalm 89
- Proverbs 14:12

But God wasn't merely promising to give Abram a big family. In Genesis 3:25, God had promised a seed who would crush the head of the serpent. That seed had not yet come, but he would come through Abram. Abram himself, however, was suffering under the curse that the serpent had brought into the world, a curse of death, a curse of barrenness. The word translated as "descendants" in Genesis 15:5 is the Hebrew word "seed," the same word used in Genesis 3:15. The author of Genesis is pointing his readers back to Genesis 3:15—the son who would become a great nation would also bring about the seed-son who would crush the head of the serpent. Abram was believing God for a son and through that son, a seed who would redeem mankind.

"And he believed in the LORD, and He accounted it to him for righteousness" (Gen 15:6). We don't

Unit 3: Abraham, Isaac and Jacob

OBJECTIVES

Feel...

- gratitude that God often makes promises that are all on His good name and don't depend on our performance.
- sadness at the way Abram's family behaved when Abram married Hagar and attempted to fulfill God's promise through her son.
- joy at Abram's restoration and new name.

Understand...

- that God passed through the dead animals, without Abram doing anything.
- that Abram believed God and God made him righteous as a result.
- that it was a sin for Abram to have a son with Hagar because it wasn't God's design for marriage.
- that Abram fell, but God redeemed his fall and continued to use him.
- that God renamed Abram from "great father" to Abraham—"father of multitudes," because He would now have to make nations out of both Ishmael and the son of promise.
- that circumcision was a sign of God's covenant with the seed-nation.
- that the ultimate result of Lot moving toward Sodom was that he lost all that he had.

Apply this understanding by...

- identifying an area where you have "fallen" already and considering how God might redeem and continue to use you.
- identifying an area in your life where God has been faithful in spite of your own "fall" and praise God for His faithfulness.

know if Abram knew exactly what all was bound up with this promise that God had made. He may well have understood that the head-crushing seed would come through him. Or, perhaps he simply believed God would give him a son who would become a great nation. Regardless, Abram believed God, and it was credited to him as righteousness. Without doing a single act of obedience, God saw Abram as righteous. This is the kind of God we have; He does not make us labor under the burden of the fall, trying desperately to eek out our own righteousness through acts of obedience. Rather, we serve a God who says, "You are righteous"—and means it—and then calls us to a life of obedience.

God then reiterated His promise that Abram would inherit the land in which he was living, the land of Canaan (Gen 15:7). Abram, perhaps becoming more bold before God, said, "Lord God, how shall I know that I will inherit it?" (Gen 15:8).

In response, God instructed Abram to perform what looks to us like an odd ritual. He told him to cut some animals in half and lay the two halves of their bodies opposite each other in a row. Abram then went to sleep and had a vision of the future of his descendants; while God, in the form of an oven and a torch, passed through the middle of the cut pieces (Gen 15:9-17).

There are a number of layers of meaning in this picture, but we want you to understand only a couple of really important points. First, when God passed through the middle of those animals, He was saying, "May I be cut up like these animals if I break my promise." By this symbolic act, God drove home the veracity of His word. Second, notice that God passed through the animals alone. There was nothing Abram had to do to receive this promise; it was all on God.

Hagar and Ishmael
Abram's faith was tested shortly after God had reiterated His promises and Abram had believed. The scene in Genesis 16:1-4 is reminiscent of Genesis 3 when Eve, being deceived by the serpent, gave the fruit to Adam, who willfully ate even through he wasn't under deception. Abram knew better than to sleep with Hagar; just look at all the ways God had affirmed His promises in Genesis 15! Nevertheless, Abram obeyed his wife anyway.

It seems strange to us, but the arrangement suggested by Sarai was actually pretty common in their culture. If a woman was unable to bear children, she would assign a servant to be a surrogate in her place, and her husband would sleep with the servant. But just because it was common, didn't make it right; they were stepping outside God's design for the family. "Everybody does it" was not a good excuse; Abram and Sarai knew better. Abram was seeking a good thing (the fulfillment of God's promise), but he was impatient and untrusting, and his lack of faith brought bad results.

Hagar didn't respond well to Sarai after she conceived; she allowed herself to harbor spite against Sarai and brought tension into their relationship (Gen 16:4). Of course, the situation itself never would have happened if it were not for Sarai asking Abram to father a child with Hagar to start with. Sarai, in turn, blamed Abram for the way Hagar was treating her, since he had slept with Hagar (Gen 16:5). Abram dodged responsibility and told Sarai to handle it however she wanted. As a result, Sarai treated Hagar harshly (which, let's not forget, Hagar was bringing on herself), and the result was that Hagar ran away (Gen 16:6). Everyone involved had a share in the blame of this family drama.

But God still had promises to keep to Abram—He had passed through those cut-up animals alone, so even though Abram had lost faith, God was faithful. He stopped Hagar from running and promised that her son would also become a great nation (Gen 16:7-12), keeping His promise to Abram and his descendants, even though Abram had sinned. (Ishmael is the father of the Arab peoples.)

God instituted circumcision
In Genesis 17, God appeared to Abram and called him to live faithfully. God didn't go back on His promise, even though Abram had been unfaithful. In fact, God reiterated and expanded His promise: "I will multiply you exceedingly... and you shall be a father of many nations" (Gen 17:2-4). This expanded promise allowed God to keep His original intention of giving Abram a son miraculously without abandoning Ishmael. In keeping with the expanded promise, God also renamed Abram, "great father," to Abraham, "father of a multitude," because God would now make him a father of *many* nations (Gen 17:5).

Now that Abraham was going to be the father of many nations, God instituted circumcision (Gen 17:10-14) to identify who was a part of the covenant bearing seed-nation whom God had chosen. Circumcision became a way to *divide* covenant sons from non-covenant sons. It is important to remember that both God's unilateral covenant promise and Abram's faith preceded circumcision.

In contrast to his faith in God when He promised him a son in Genesis 15, Abraham laughed in his heart when God promised yet again that He would give him a son miraculously (Gen 17:17). Abraham wanted Ishmael to be the son of promise, but God had a different plan. In spite of Abraham's lack of faith, God would be good to His word.

Unit 3: Abraham, Isaac and Jacob

APPLICATION

God is faithful to His word. God made a promise to Abraham, and He kept His promise even though Abraham failed all along the way. In fact, God redeemed Abraham's mistakes. The story of Abraham is a crucial turning point in the big Story of the Bible, and God worked within Abraham's mistakes to bring about His good purposes in the long run. How much more can God redeem our mistakes to work within His plan? God *can and does* redeem the mistakes we make to bring about His purpose. However, we may still have to suffer the consequences of the sin, just like Abraham, his family, and the entire nation of Israel suffered the consequences of Abraham's (and Sarah's) sin. Can you think of a time you made a sinful mistake that God brought good out of? Did it still cost you something?

ACTIVITIES

1. The Magnitude of God's Promise. God makes ridiculously fantastic promises that no one should ever believe; except that they are true. God promised Abraham descendants that were as many as the number of stars in the sky. When you look up at the stars in the city, you only see a small fraction of the stars that are actually there; the rest are obscured by the lights of the city. Do a Google image search for "panoramic night sky" and look at some of the images, be sure to expand the pictures to their full size and pan around to get a feel for how many stars Abraham might have seen. Reflect on the amazing promise God gave to Abraham and write a paragraph below thanking God for His goodness. _____

_____

_____

_____

To take it a step further, do a Google image search for "Hubble ultra deep field". This photo, taken by the Hubble telescope, shows a bit of the sky that is the size of a grain of sand held at arms length and has thousands of galaxies in it, each with billions of stars. God's creation is truly staggering, as are His promises. List the parallels between Abram's life and Israel's later history. when he and his wife were too old to have children! Write a prayer thanking God for His unending goodness._____

_____

_____

_____

Lesson 3.2

2. Journal Time: God's Faithfulness When We Fail. God was faithful to Abraham, even after he failed by doubting God's promise to him and having a son with Hagar. Think of a time when you doubted God and failed Him. Write about this situation in the space below, thanking God for His faithfulness in the midst of your failures and recognizing that God continues to use you, just like He did Abraham, even when you fall. _____

_____

_____

_____

_____

EVALUATION

1. What was significant about God putting Abram to sleep and crossing between the split carcasses alone? _____

_____

2. What does the name Abram mean? _____

3. What does the name Abraham mean? _____

4. What happened between Genesis 15 and Genesis 17 that required a change of name for Abram?

_____

_____

5. What did circumcision mean to Abraham and his household? _____

_____

_____

6. What did it mean when God took counsel with Abraham before destroying Sodom and Gomorrah?

_____

_____

7. What happened to Lot as a result of moving closer and eventually into Sodom? _____

_____

_____

LESSON 3.3

God Fulfilled His Promise: The Seed-Son Born and Protected from Two Threats

THE STORY

Lesson Theme - God fulfilled His promise and protected the seed-son.

God had promised Abram a son, and God was good to His word. In Genesis 21, Isaac, the son of promise, is born. However, both before and after the birth of the seed-son, the seed-line was threatened. First, Abimelech took Sarah as a wife, potentially cutting Abraham off; then, after Isaac was born, Ishmael posed a threat to the promised seed-son.

Abimelech and the seed-line

After Sodom and Gomorrah were destroyed, Abraham moved to the land of the Philistines and lived in the city of Gerar (Gen 20:1). Abraham made exactly the mistake that Lot had made when he moved toward Sodom and then into the city. And, like Lot, Abraham was willing to give up something to make peace with Gerar. Just like he had done in Egypt, he told Abimelech that Sarah was his sister, and Abimelech took her as his wife (Gen 20:2).

God appeared to Abimelech and threatened him—he would die if he didn't return Abraham's wife (Gen 20:3-7). Abimelech was eager to do just that, so God spared his life.

This lesson's passage closes with Abimelech making a peace treaty with Abraham (Gen 21:22-32), which appears to have been his intention all along. He took Sarah as a wife, but never consummated the marriage (Gen 20:6); apparently, he had her as his wife for some time, because there was enough time for Abimelech and his people to notice that their women were unable to conceive (Gen 20:18). It seems that Abimelech's marriage to Sarah was meant to be a political marriage to start with. In that day and time the effect of such a marriage would be enduring peace between Abraham and Abimelech.

We find out in Genesis 20:13 that Abraham had made an agreement with Sarah from the very beginning that she would say he was her brother wherever they went. It was Abraham's way of making peace and ensuring his safety in foreign lands. But Abraham's strategy didn't work out nearly as well as God's strategy. God was protecting His seed-line, and Abraham's attempt to do it himself only backfired.

OVERVIEW

The seed-line was continually being threatened, but God protected it. Abraham tried to protect his family by lying about his relationship with Sarah, but he was caught. God protected Abraham from Abimelech far better than Abraham could ever have protected himself. Ishmael posed a different sort of threat that Abraham couldn't see, but God protected Isaac's inheritance, while also protecting Ishmael and Hagar.

SOURCE MATERIAL

- Genesis 20-21
- Psalm 56
- Proverbs 16:7

Unit 3: Abraham, Isaac and Jacob

OBJECTIVES

Feel...

- indignation that Abraham didn't trust God to protect him.
- joyful admiration (laughter) for God fulfilling His promise to Abraham and Sarah when they were too old to have children.
- admiration that Abraham could trust God with Hagar and Ishmael.

Understand...

- the threats that Abimelech and Ishmael each posed to the seed-line.
- that Isaac's birth was the beginning of the fulfillment of God's promise to make Abraham a great nation.
- that Abraham was showing both lack of faith (conceiving Ishmael, lying about his relationship with Sarah) and great faith (trusting God with Hagar and Ishmael's fate).
- that God was at work in fulfilling the promises He made to Abraham in Genesis 12. (Even when Abraham messed up the process, God redeemed it.)

Apply this understanding by...

- identifying past areas where God gave you something good that you had failed to obtain for yourself.
- considering whether there are present areas in your life where you need to trust God's promise instead of just trying to get things done yourself.
- identifying and praising God for times when He has redeemed your mistakes, turning them into a part of His story of victory in your life.

Isaac born and Ishmael sent away
In time, God "visited Sarah" and she conceived and gave birth to a son (Gen 21:1). In obedience to God, Abraham circumcised and named his son Isaac. The promised seed had come. The promised seed-son always comes. Abraham and Sarah's joy was unspeakable.

Notice the role that laughter has played in the events leading up to Isaac's birth and in the fulfillment of the promise. In Genesis 17:17 Abraham laughed to himself about the ridiculousness of God's promise, and Sarah did the same in Genesis 18:12. Now Sarah laughed when Isaac was born, but this time not in mockery, but with joy. Sarah foretold that those who heard the story of Isaac's birth would laugh with her (Gen 21:6). We should join in joyous laughter at the gracious fulfillment of God's promise in giving the seed-son Isaac. This was the first of a number of miraculous births associated with the seed-line. And, appropriately, Isaac's name means, "he laughs."

Ishmael was loved by his father. Abraham cared for him and initially wanted him to inherit the promise (Gen 17:18), but God wouldn't do it. Ultimately, Abraham's two sons couldn't both live in the same area and share an inheritance. That, Sarah knew, would lead only to problems (Gen 21:10). And as much as Abraham didn't like it (Gen 21:11), Sarah was right.

Abraham didn't want to send Ishmael away, but God told him to listen to Sarah, so he arose early in the morning, gave Hagar bread and a skin of water, and sent her out into the wilderness with her son (Gen 21:13-15). Her chances of survival—by herself, with a small child in the desert, having no animals for food or transportation—were not good to say the least, and Abraham knew it. But God had promised Abraham that He would make Ishmael into a great nation. This was the *first* time God asked Abraham to surrender his son, and he trusted God to fulfill His promise. God was training Abraham for later when God would ask him to surrender the promised seed, Isaac, in a *much* more difficult way.

There is an important ongoing theme in this lesson. Abraham's faithfulness was less than perfect, but God continued His plan to fulfill His promises in spite of Abraham's failures. Several times now we have seen God redeeming situations that Abraham had messed up. (We saw this with Abraham acting as though Sarah was his sister in Egypt, then in the birth of Ishmael, and finally here with Abimelech.) In each case, God turned Abraham's mess-ups into a part of the story of victory and a part of the fulfillment to promises already made (see Gen 12 again). God does the same in our lives.

APPLICATION

In the previous lesson, Abraham tried to fulfill God's promise for him by sleeping with Hagar, his wife's servant. Then, in this lesson, Abraham tried to protect himself and his family by telling Abimelech that Sarah was his sister. Instead of protecting him, this lie led to the potential loss of his wife and therefore, the loss of the seed-line. Abraham kept trying to help God, and it only made things worse.

This is the nature of a lack of trust—when we try to get what God wants to give us on our own strength, it only hurts us. Instead of trying to push our way into God's will, we can simply receive God's blessing by holding out our hands and waiting.

ACTIVITIES

1. God's Good Gifts. In the space below describe a time when you tried to get something good for yourself (a toy, a trip somewhere, whatever) and failed—but then God gave it to you anyway, in a different way that had nothing to do with what you'd done to try to get it yourself. _____

_____
_____
_____
_____
_____
_____
_____
_____

Unit 3: Abraham, Isaac and Jacob

2. Personal Reflection: Laughter. Abraham and Sarah named their son Isaac, which means laughter. Answer the following questions .

Why did Abraham and Sarah name their son Isaac? Why did they laugh? _____

_____

_____

_____

_____

How was this laughter different from the last time we learned about Abraham and Sarah laughing? ___

_____

_____

_____

When was the last time you felt so delighted by what God had done that you laughed? _____

_____

_____

_____

_____

_____

_____

Is it possible that there are things happening all around us that we should be delighted by, and we just don't see them? Give some examples. _____

_____

_____

_____

_____

_____

_____

Lesson 3.3

EVALUATION

1. When Abraham lived in Abimelech's land, was it true that someone could have tried to kill Abraham and take Sarah? _____

2. Why didn't Abraham need to worry about someone trying to kill him and take Sarah? _____
_____
_____

3. Since Abraham was in danger, was he justified in lying about Sarah and saying she was his sister?
_____

4. Why did Abraham and Sarah name their son Isaac? _____
_____
_____

5. What was the threat that Ishmael posed to Isaac? What did Sarah see that Abraham did not? _____
_____
_____
_____

6. Was Abraham right or wrong in sending Hagar and Ishmael out on their own with so few provisions? _____
_____
_____
_____

7. At the end of Genesis 21, Abimelech went out of his way to make sure there was peace between him and Abraham. Why did he do this? _____
_____
_____
_____
_____

LESSON 3.4

God Tested and Evaluated Abraham: Abraham Offered Isaac and a Substitute Provided

UNIT 3

THE STORY

Lesson Theme - God evaluated Abraham
God created the heavens and the earth through a fourfold process: He commanded, divided, named and evaluated. We have seen God's fourfold pattern of creative activity through the story of Abraham as God created the seed-nation. God **commanded** (called) Abram out of Ur and **divided** him from his own people and from Lot (Gen 12-13). Then, God validated Abram's name with a covenant in Genesis 15 and **renamed** him in Genesis 17. In this lesson, we see Abraham tested and **evaluated** (Gen 22-23).

God had given Abraham a son, and now He was going to ask him to give that son back. In Genesis 22:1, God appeared to Abraham and called his name, to which Abraham responded, "Here I am." Abraham had demonstrated an ability to respond to God in quick obedience before (for example, when God called him out of Ur in Genesis 12), but Abraham had also shown a lack of faith in God's ability to provide the promised seed-son through his wife Sarah. In this story, God tested Abraham in exactly the area where he had shown himself to be weakest. Abraham had desired a son, and God had given him one. How would Abraham respond when God called him to give that son back to Him? With quick obedience! "So Abraham rose early in the morning and saddled his donkey" (Gen 22:3).

Abraham knew two things about this situation: (1) he was supposed to sacrifice Isaac, and (2) Isaac would become a great nation. Apparently, Abraham believed that God would raise Isaac

OVERVIEW

God tested Abraham by commanding him to go to Mount Moriah to offer his promised son Isaac as an ascension offering. Abraham responded with quick obedience and traveled to Moriah with his son and some servants. He left his servants at the base of the mount, declaring that both he and Isaac would return; he believed God would raise Isaac from the dead. When Abraham was about to kill his son, God provided a substitute lamb. God then evaluated Abraham and rewarded him for his obedience with promises of descendants and an inheritance. Later, Sarah died, and Abraham bought a piece of land from the Canaanites as a burial plot for her.

SOURCE MATERIAL

- Genesis 22-23
- Hebrews 11:17-19
- Psalm 105
- Proverbs 13:1

from the dead, which nicely solves the incompatibility of those two pieces of information. Abraham's belief is explicit in Hebrews 11:17-19, but it's implicit here in the Genesis story. In Genesis 22:5, Abraham told his servants, "*We* will come back to you." When Isaac asked about the sacrifice, Abraham told him that God would provide. It may be that Abraham was a little fuzzy on the details of how God was going to work the whole thing out, but he was sure that God would take

Unit 3: Abraham, Isaac and Jacob

OBJECTIVES

Feel...

- impressed with Abraham's quick obedience.
- impressed with Abraham and Isaac's faith that God would raise Isaac from the dead and provide a substitute.
- gratitude to God for saving Isaac and providing a substitute.

Understand...

- that Abraham was quick to obey God in a challenging act of faith and obedience.
- that Abraham and Isaac both believed God would raise Isaac from the dead.
- that Isaac was both a representative of Christ (he offered himself willingly) and a picture of humanity (God provided a substitute so that he didn't have to die).
- that, because of Abraham's faith and quick obedience, God reaffirmed His promises to Abraham and gave him a positive evaluation.

Apply this understanding by...

- identifying at least one area in your life where you need to obey sacrificially (like Isaac did).
- preparing to obey in that area with no hesitation at all (like Abraham did).

care of it and that, in the end, Isaac would be alive and capable of fulfilling the promise.

We don't know exactly how old Isaac was at this time, but we do know he was old enough and strong enough to haul all the wood for the sacrifice up the mountain (Gen 22:6). Yet he willingly allowed his father to lay him on the wood and raise the knife over him without a fight. The seed-son willingly offered himself as a sacrifice in obedience to his father, as Jesus would later do.

At the same time (looking through another lens), Isaac is the picture of fallen humanity, rescued from death by God providing a lamb as a substitute.

God evaluated Abraham and reiterated His promises to him. Would God have made Abraham a great nation and fulfilled His other promises to him even if he had not willingly offered Isaac? Yes, because God had already promised this unconditionally. But Abraham had lived up to what God promised him; he had walked worthy of his calling, to borrow a phrase from the New Testament (Eph 4:1). The point is that God could now fulfill His promises *because of* Abraham's faithfulness, instead of fulfilling them *in spite of* Abraham's sin. The latter would, of course, have been much less glorious and satisfying for Abraham personally. (For an example of how God fulfilled His promises in spite of a person's sin, look at how God handled His promises to David after David's sin with Bathsheba and Uriah.)

The faithfulness Abraham displayed on the mountain came to define his whole life. Notice that much later, when Abraham buried Sarah, he *bought* a plot of land. He had been a nomad and lived his whole life as a nomad in the land God promised to give to him and his descendants. Sarah's tomb was the only piece of land *he actually owned* within the promised land. Knowing that the whole land would one day belong to his people, Abraham trusted God's promise and bought a cemetery plot. Joseph exhibited similar faith later on—see Genesis 50:24-25 and Hebrews 11:22.

APPLICATION

Abraham provides us with a model of how we should obey—quickly and fully, even if it looks like it might hurt. Of course, obeying God sometimes does hurt, but never as much as not obeying Him. Is there an area in your life where you are called to imitate Isaac and Jesus and act sacrificially? How can you obey quickly and without hesitation like Abraham did?

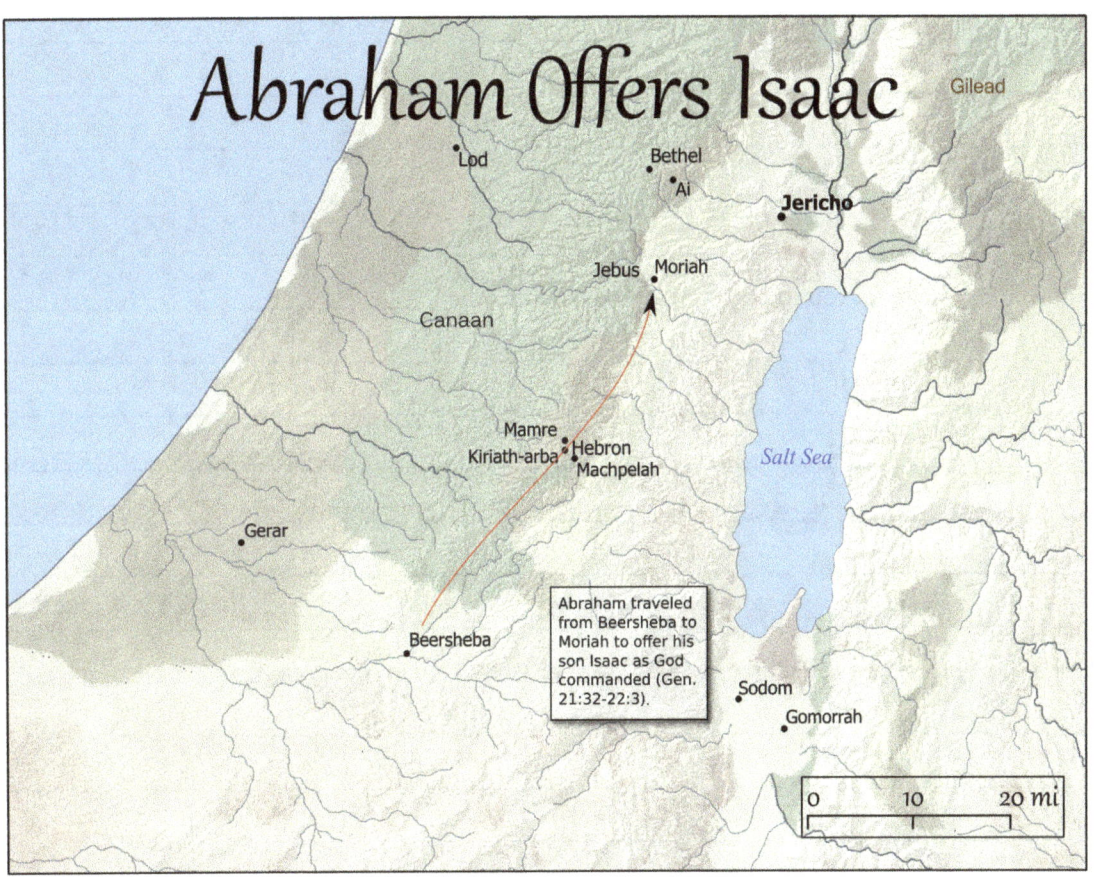

Unit 3: Abraham, Isaac and Jacob

ACTIVITIES

1. Journal Time: Sacrifice. In the space below, answer the following.

Identify an area in your life where you can be a sacrifice for the sake of others. This does not have to be something big and complicated; it could simply be doing something kind for a friend in need.

What would it mean for you to obey God quickly in that area?

Write a short prayer you could pray everyday to seek God's help in that area.

Lesson 3.4

EVALUATION

1. Why did God ask Abraham to offer Isaac as an ascension offering? _____
_____

How did Abraham respond? _____
_____

2. God had promised that a nation would come from Isaac; how was Abraham able to offer Isaac on the altar and still believe that God would fulfill His promise? _____
_____

3. How do you suppose Isaac felt about being offered on the altar?_____
_____
_____

4. Isaac is a picture of both Jesus Christ and humanity. How is he a picture of each of these? _____
_____
_____

5. How did God respond to Abraham's faithfulness? _____
_____
_____

6. What was the significance of Abraham owning Sarah's tomb?_____
_____
_____
_____

LESSON 3.5

Isaac and Rebekah: The Chosen Son Married and Came of Age

UNIT 3

THE STORY

Lesson Theme - Isaac became a man.
In the culture of Isaac's day, the task of finding a wife had very little to do with a man's own desires; parents found matches for their children. So Abraham tasked a trusted servant with the job. The servant, in turn, trusted in God, and God delivered in a spectacular way.

Abraham was old (Gen 24:1); he was not capable of finding a wife for Isaac at this point in his life, so he made his servant promise to find a wife from among his own family and bring her back for Isaac. Abraham tried to strike a balance between two concerns. He didn't want Isaac to take a wife from among the Canaanites in the land where they currently lived. For one, the Canaanites were exceedingly wicked, and Abraham knew that a marriage alliance between his family and the Canaanites would bring that wickedness into his family. Furthermore, God had specifically told Abraham that his family would be taken to Egypt, then return to the land and take possession of the land of the Canaanites. Creating marital alliances with them would only undermine God's promise that His people would supplant the Canaanites.

Abraham's other concern was that, once he had found a wife from among his own family, Isaac would want to settle in his family's land. God had called Abraham to leave his home to go to the land of promise. It would be counter to God's purposes for Isaac to return to the place God had called his father out of.

OVERVIEW

After spending his first 40 years as a single man in his father's house, Isaac came into his own. He married, came to be at peace with his half-brother Ishmael and started a family. God blessed him and made him great. This lead to his neighbors in the land making a peace treaty with him.

SOURCE MATERIAL

- Genesis 24-26
- Hebrews 12:14-17
- Psalm 112
- Proverbs 31:10-31, esp. verses 15, 17, 25

The servant questioned Abraham on this point, asking him if he should just bring Isaac back to the land of Abraham's family if he couldn't find a woman who was willing to move away from her family in order to marry Isaac (Gen 24:5). Abraham made it clear that the priority was that the servant should not bring Isaac back there, and the servant would be released from his oath if he didn't find a woman willing to come back with him (Gen 24:8).

Then the servant, obedient to Abraham, went on his way with ten camels and all sorts of gifts (Gen 24:10). When he came to Mesopotamia, the land of Abraham's family, he sat down by a well and prayed to the Lord. He asked God to show him in a very specific way the woman Isaac was to marry; he asked that she would offer to draw

Unit 3: Abraham, Isaac and Jacob

OBJECTIVES

Feel...

- admiration for the faith shown by the servant and Rebekah, for Rebekah's sheer physical strength and stamina, and for her willingness to do hard work.
- surprise that Esau would sell his birthright for a bowl of soup.
- irritation that Isaac repeated Abraham's mistake in lying about his wife.

Understand...

- how God repeated with Isaac (in a different way) what He did with Abraham: separated him from his father's house, and made him great.
- that Abraham's mantle, his status as head of the seed-line, had passed on to Isaac.
- that Isaac's mantle would, in turn, pass to Jacob, especially once Esau chose to sell his birthright.

Apply this understanding by...

- identifying the hard work in your own life that you are tempted to shirk.
- doing that hard work faithfully, as unto the Lord.
- trusting God to bring good results from this hard work.

water not only for him, but also for his camels (Gen 24:12-14).

The servant's request had to be really extraordinary, otherwise what good would it be as a sign? And extraordinary it was. The amount camels drink varies by season, but an adult camel in warm weather can drink up to 50 gallons in a day. We know from Genesis 24:10 that the servant came with ten loaded camels. Say the camels only drank half as much as they could—that's still 250 gallons of water (over 2,000 lbs)! And every last drop had to be pulled up out of the well by hand, with a bucket and a rope.

But God heard the servant's prayer, and it happened just as he had asked. Before he had even finished praying, a beautiful woman named Rebekah arrived with a pitcher on her shoulder (Gen 24:15). He asked if she would draw him some water, and she volunteered to draw water for all his camels as well (Gen 24:19). Rebekah was *seriously* strong.

The servant then offered her some gifts, found out who she was, and she ran all the way home to tell her family (Gen 24:22-28).

Rebekah's family handled the situation well. Once they had heard the story from the servant, they invited him into their home. The servant told them Abraham's instructions on finding a wife for Isaac, then explained his prayer and the clear answer the Lord gave when Rebekah arrived at the well. Rebekah's family understood the sign that God had given, correctly discerned God's will for the situation, and were willing to go along with it (Gen 24:34-60).

The Genesis text tells the rest of the incident with little fanfare. Rebekah and the servant returned; Isaac and Rebekah met and married.

Abraham continued to trust God with his promised son. Because Isaac inherited the promises, he would also eventually inherit the promised land. Abraham knew that if his other sons lived in the land, they and their descendants would eventually be supplanted (Abraham had six other

Unit 3: Abraham, Isaac and Jacob

sons by Keturah—Gen 25:2). Trusting God to fulfill His promises to Isaac, Abraham sent his other sons to the east.

Abraham died and Isaac and Rebekah started a family
Abraham died, and Isaac and Ishmael—both desert kings in their own right—came together in peace to bury him (Gen 25:8-9). The account then gives us the genealogy of Ishmael (Gen 25:12-18). Isaac had now come into his own. His parents had died, he had found a wife (and such a wife!), he was at peace with his brothers and dwelling in the land. All he needed now was offspring.

But there was a problem. Rebekah had been barren for 20 years (see Gen 25:20, 26), which is important to mention, because the barren woman who eventually gives birth to the promised son is a major theme in the Bible. Rebekah eventually conceived as a result of Isaac's prayers (Gen 25:21).

Jacob, Esau and the birthright
Rebekah's pregnancy was troubled, because the twin boys within her womb were fighting even before they were born (Gen 25:22). God told Rebekah that two nations were struggling within her, a prophecy that was borne out in the manner of their birth (Gen 25:23-26). The twins' struggle extended to their parents, with Isaac favoring Esau, and Rebekah favoring Jacob.

"The older shall serve the younger" (Gen 25:23) is another common theme in the Bible. It's possibly a typological shadow of Cain's failure. (The original older brother slew his younger brother; periodically thereafter God reminded older brothers that this was a bad idea by promoting the younger brother.)

The story then turns us to a key episode in Isaac's family's life which highlights the relationship between the brothers: Esau selling his birthright. This story is often told with Jacob as the bad guy, withholding food from a starving Esau in order to extort the birthright from him. However, within this story and in other biblical commentary on it, Esau is the one painted as the bad guy for despising what was his by right (see Gen 25:34, Heb 12:14-17).

As the firstborn son, the birthright belonged to Esau and included a double portion of the inheritance. Within Hebrew inheritance customs, the estate was divided equally among the sons, except that the oldest son got twice as much as anyone else. So in this case, Esau stood to inherit two thirds of Isaac's estate, and he gave up this double portion to Jacob. The birthright was not all a bed of roses, however. It also included responsibility to care for the father's widow, the responsibility to lead the family, and so on.

We don't know why Esau took his birthright so lightly. Perhaps he was doing so well for himself that he felt no interest in inheriting from his father. Or perhaps he didn't want the responsibility that went with it. In any case, the Scriptures make it clear that Esau was wrong to despise his birthright.

Isaac's dealings with Abimelech
The final element in our story of how Isaac came of age regards his relations with the peoples of the land. There was a famine in the land, and God took the opportunity to make Isaac the same promises He had once made to Abraham (Gen 26:1-5). Isaac, guided by the Lord, returned to Philistia, the land of Abimelech where Abraham had once lived for many years. Isaac had learned Abraham's trick of lying about his wife and repeated it (Gen 26:7); and Isaac got caught

in his lie, just like his dad had (Gen 26:9). Isaac was wrong to lie about his wife; he ought to have trusted God's promise to bless him (not get him killed) in the land where God told him to dwell. As it turned out, Abimelech meant to do right by Isaac all along and made his good intentions clear to Isaac by the way he responded when he found out about Isaac's lie.

Despite Isaac's lack of trust, God blessed him, greatly multiplying his possessions and his power. Notice that the Philistines asked Isaac to leave because he was mightier than they were (Gen 26:16). Isaac was not some tattered nomad with a pup tent and a couple of camels. As with Abraham and later Jacob, Isaac was a mighty desert king, with a large following of servants. (And by servants, think "knights" as well as "butlers." Many of the servants would have been strong people in their own right who found it to their advantage to live with Isaac.)

Notice that Isaac, despite his power, would rather move and dig another well than go to war over water rights (Gen 26:15-22). He continued moving until *the Lord* made room for him in the land.

As he had with Abraham, Abimelech saw the prosperity God had given Isaac and wanted to make a treaty with him (Gen 26:28-29). This demonstrates, better than anything else could, that Isaac had come into his own. He was blessed by God to the point that it was worth it for a *country* to make a peace treaty with him.

APPLICATION

God blesses kindness and diligence. We can't make things happen in our own effort, but often God uses our effort to bring about great things for His glory. This may sound confusing, but look at Rebekah. She didn't know that serving Abraham's servant at the well would get her a husband, or that as a result, she would play a key role in bringing the seed-nation and ultimately the Messiah into the world. But her faithful kindness and obedience brought about those things.

Working hard, obeying God, and being kind always pays off—and often in ways we might not expect. What is God calling you to do? Where does He want you to work harder or show more kindness? Obey and see what the Lord does with your obedience.

ACTIVITIES

1. Journal Time. Spend some time reflecting in the space below about the following questions.

Rebekah was a hard worker, and God blessed her with a husband who became a king. Are you a hard worker?_____

_____

Where are you dodging hard work that you ought to be doing? _____

_____

Lesson 3.5

What are some ways you can start working hard like Rebekah did? _____
_____

3. Personal Reflection. Reflect on the story by answering the following questions.

Why would Esau sell his birthright for a bowl of soup? _____
_____

Why did Isaac favor Esau and Rebekah favor Jacob? _____
_____

Is it a good idea for parents to love one child more than another? _____

EVALUATION

1. Isaac and Ishmael came together to bury their father Abraham. What did their actions indicate? ___
_____

2. How did the servant know that Rebekah was the right woman for Isaac? _____
_____

3. What happened so that Rebekah was able to become pregnant? _____
_____

4. Who loved Esau more, and who loved Jacob more? _____
_____

5. What did Esau give up to Jacob for a bowl of soup? _____

6. When Isaac moved to Abimelech's land, why did he feel the need to lie that Rebekah was his sister?
_____

7. Was it necessary for Isaac to lie about Rebekah being his sister when he moved to Abimelech's land? _____
_____

8. Why did the Philistines ask Isaac to leave their land? _____
_____
_____

LESSON 3.6

Jacob, Esau, and the Birthright: The Second Son Received the Blessing as God Promised

UNIT 3

THE STORY

Lesson Theme - Isaac attempted to subvert God's plan.
This story is commonly taught with Rebekah and Jacob as the bad guys, wickedly deceiving Isaac in order to steal Esau's blessing. While the text does not comment on whether Rebekah and Jacob's motives were pure, we do know that their actions were in harmony with God's will. God had already revealed before Jacob and Esau were born that the older (Esau) would serve the younger (Jacob) (Gen 25:23). The blessing that Isaac was trying to give Esau (and mistakenly gave to Jacob) included, "Be master over your brethren, and let your mother's sons bow down to you" (Gen 27:29b). In other words, Isaac was trying to overrule God. So the bad guys in the first part of this story were not Jacob or Rebekah, but Isaac, who was refusing to follow God's will, and Esau, who was going along with it. (For an example of what Esau ought to have done in this situation, look forward to how Jonathan behaved when his father Saul tried to eliminate God's chosen successor [David] so that Jonathan could inherit.)

Jacob and Rebekah conspired to take the blessing from Esau
Thourought the Story, we are tracking the chosen seed-line through Scripture. One aspect of the seed-line is the ruling blessing that gets passed down from generation to generation. Noah had given this blessing to Shem in Genesis 9:26, and though his words of blessing are not recorded, Abraham blessed Isaac as his primary heir (Gen 25:5-6).

OVERVIEW

God said before Jacob and Esau were born that the older would serve the younger, but Isaac favored Esau and tried to give him the ruling blessing anyway. Rebekah sided with God and ensured that Jacob received the blessing, but as a result, Jacob had to go into exile for his own safety. Seeing himself losing ground, Esau tried to regain favor with his parents by taking yet another wife.

SOURCE MATERIAL

- Genesis 27-28
- Psalm 133
- Proverbs 6:16-19, 21:30

Isaac was getting old and could barely see; he knew it was time pass the blessing on to his son. But instead of blessing his younger son, the one whom God had chosen, Isaac decided to bless his favored son Esau.

Before he blessed Esau, Jacob asked him to kill some game and prepare him a meal. Isaac and Rebekah had been quite close up to this point; Genesis 24:67 says they were well-bonded for decades before this part of the story. But the favorite game, played by both Isaac and Rebekah, drove a wedge between them. So when Rebekah heard Isaac ask Esau to make him a meal so he could bless him, she conspired with Jacob to trick her husband.

Unit 3: Abraham, Isaac and Jacob

OBJECTIVES

Feel...

- amazed that Isaac would try to outmaneuver God.
- empathy with Jacob and Esau, who had to live with the results of their father's sin.

Understand...

- that whatever their personal motives, Rebekah and Jacob were acting in harmony with God's revealed will, while Isaac and Esau were trying to thwart it.
- that Isaac's failure made the relationship between Jacob and Esau even worse than it was before and endangered Jacob's life.

Apply this understanding by...

- considering where you are attempting to thwart God's revealed will and repenting of your sin.
- considering in what ways you can sow peace instead of discord between yourself and your siblings (or between siblings in other families if you have no siblings).

So, Rebekah made a stew that would taste like one Esau would have made, and Jacob dressed up in animal hides to imitate Esau's hairy skin.

The possibility that Jacob might try to trick him to take the blessing from Esau was not lost on Isaac. When Jacob brought the stew to his father, Isaac knew enough to test and see if it was really Esau (Gen 27:21-27). Isaac's first test was explicit (feeling his hands), but he still wasn't sure. He went ahead and ate the meal and then asked for a kiss, but what he really wanted was to smell his son's clothing. When he smelled Esau's clothing, he was convinced and gave his blessing.

The nature of the blessing itself reveals the extent of Isaac's rebellion against God. God had already said that the older would serve the younger, but Isaac was trying to make Esau the inheritor.

Isaac's blessing had real authority. It couldn't be taken back even though Isaac had been tricked; it couldn't be undone. Notice how Isaac talked about his blessing of Jacob in Genesis 27:37: "I have made him your master...with grain and wine I have sustained him." Isaac's blessing of future grain and wine was as good as giving Jacob grain and wine; it was something Jacob could take to the bank. This blessing wasn't just Isaac's good wishes that might or might not come true; God was going to heed Isaac's words, and all parties concerned knew it.

The authority of the blessing made Isaac's next action a much greater crime. Isaac couldn't reverse his blessing and couldn't give ruling power to Esau, but he could still alter the situation. The blessing he gave Esau provided sustenance (no problem there), but it also guaranteed continued animosity between the brothers and promised Esau success in overthrowing his brother (Gen 27:39-40). *This blessing had just as much authority as the blessing upon Jacob; it was guaranteed to happen.* Instead of healing the rift between his sons, Isaac cemented Esau's status as a rebel against God's chosen custodian of the seed-line. (Contrast Isaac's actions with the way Abraham handled his other sons so as to keep them all at peace with Isaac.)

And in fact, the rebellion started immediately. Esau was content to live with Jacob as the heir apparent only because he had already decided to kill Jacob as soon as Isaac died (Gen 27:41); and Isaac's blessing, if not exactly promising success to the assassination attempt, guaranteed at least that Esau wouldn't have to live under Jacob's rule. (Notice the shades of Cain and Abel here: the older brother wanting to murder the younger brother because God favored him.)

Not wanting to lose her sons, Rebekah prepared Jacob for exile and then made the case to Isaac that he needed to send Jacob away (Gen 27:42-46). Notice that *she did not tell Isaac about Esau's plan to murder Jacob*; she gave Isaac another reason to send Jacob away. Esau's wives were already a grief of mind to both parents (Gen 26:34-35), so she made a case that Jacob needed to go away and get a better wife from among their own people and not from the Canaanites. This was an argument Isaac could certainly understand; after all, it was how he got Rebekah, many years ago.

When Isaac sent Jacob to find a wife, he blessed him, and in this blessing showed that he had repented and was finally submitting to God's will for his sons. He passed on "the blessing of Abraham" to Jacob, willingly (Gen 28:4) Then, Jacob went on his way.

Esau never really had his mother's favor, and now he saw that his father had sent Jacob off to find a wife of whom both parents would approve. He had to know that his parents couldn't stand his two wives. And so, hoping to win some favor back, he took a third wife, this one from among his own people—Mahalath the daughter of Ishmael (Gen 28:6-9).

APPLICATION

Isaac knew well that Jacob was the son whom God had chosen, and he should have intentionally blessed him. Instead, he tried to outmaneuver God. Proverbs 21:30 says "There is no wisdom or understanding or counsel against the LORD." This proverb certainly proved true with Isaac; though he tried to bless Esau, God made sure that Jacob received the blessing.

God successfully carried out His plans to bless Jacob, despite Isaac's sin; nevertheless, Isaac's attempts to get in God's way brought damage to his family. His disobedience to God created division in his family and ultimately, set the nations that would come from his two sons against each other.

Are there areas of your life where you are resisting the will of God? Don't deceive yourself, it is only going to hurt you and those around you in the end.

ACTIVITIES

1. Personal Reflection. Reflect on the story by answering the following questions.

Was the alternate blessing that Isaac gave Esau really a blessing, or was it a curse? Explain your answer._____

Unit 3: Abraham, Isaac and Jacob

_____
_____
_____

Jacob had earlier bought Esau's birthright for a bowl of soup. Would he actually be able to inherit it?
_____
_____
_____

2. Alternate History Activity. Choose one of the following scenarios and write in the space below how history might have been different if people had chosen to behave differently.

1. What if Esau had a better character and Isaac had been content with God's will for his sons? What might their family have been like then?_____
_____
_____
_____

2. What if Rebekah had chosen not to go behind Isaac's back? What might have happened?_____
_____
_____

3. Journal Time: My Alternate History. This activity is a follow up to the previous activity. Let's bring it home a bit. Think back to the last time you had a dispute with a relative or someone in authority over you. In the space below, write a paragraph explaining what might have happened if you had found a way to make peace instead of contributing to the fight. _____
_____
_____
_____
_____
_____
_____

Lesson 3.6

How could you reach out to make peace now and try to undo some of the damage? Once you've thought of a way, why don't you go ahead and do it, tonight? _____
_____
_____

EVALUATION

1. Whom had God chosen to carry on the seed-line, Jacob or Esau? _____

2. In the story of Jacob and Esau, whose sin created the whole bad situation? _____
_____

3. What finally convinced Isaac that Jacob was really Esau, so that Isaac gave his blessing? _____
_____

4. What blessing did Isaac mistakenly give Jacob? _____
_____

5. Did Isaac's alternate blessing upon Esau help heal the relationship between Jacob and Esau, or did it make it worse? _____
_____
_____

6. How did Rebekah convince Isaac to send Jacob away? _____
_____
_____
_____

7. Was the reason Rebekah gave Isaac to send Jacob away really why she wanted to send Jacob away?
_____
_____
_____

8. Why did Esau marry Mahalath? _____
_____
_____

LESSON 3.7

Jacob Prepared in Exile

THE STORY

Lesson Theme - Jacob refined in exile before returning to the land of promise

This story is about Jacob's coming of age. Unlike Isaac, Jacob did not have the luxury of coming of age in his father's house; he had to live with his extended family because his brother Esau wanted to kill him. At the beginning of this story, Jacob had so little that he slept with a rock for a pillow, and God promised to make him great (Gen 28:10-15). By the end of this story, God had kept His promise, and brought Jacob back out of Laban's house safely.

Jacob left Canaan alone and in a hurry, fearing for his life. Isaac had told him to find a wife in his home country, just like Abraham had sent a servant to find a wife for Isaac. And, just as Abraham's servant met Rebekah at a well, Jacob met Rachel at a well (Gen 29:9-10). This motif continues throughout the Old Testament—when a man meets a woman at a well, there's going to be a wedding. Keep an eye out for this theme; you'll see it again.

After meeting Rachel, Jacob was immediately invited to be a part of Laban's household (Gen 29:13-14). Notice the hospitality that Laban extended to Jacob in the beginning. At first, the two men were friends, and Laban was glad to take Jacob in. For his part, Jacob pitched in and worked for Laban. After Jacob had been with Laban for a month, Laban decided he couldn't keep Jacob around for free and offered to pay him (Gen 29:15).

OVERVIEW

Jacob left his father's house as a poor refugee, but God promised to bless him and make him great. Despite Laban constantly trying to cheat Jacob, God's word came to pass, and He brought Jacob out of Laban's house with a large family and great wealth.

SOURCE MATERIAL

- Genesis 29-31
- Psalm 15
- Proverbs 11:1

Jacob wanted to marry Laban's daughter, Rachel, as his wages and was willing to work seven years for her (Gen 29:18). Laban agreed, and Jacob worked the seven years. Laban threw the wedding feast, but tricked Jacob and gave him Leah, Rachel's older sister, instead (Gen 29:23). Laban was able to trick Jacob in this way because the custom was for the bride to be *completely* veiled until the wedding night (cf. Gen 24:65). Jacob would've felt incredibly betrayed in the morning. But that's not all; image how Leah must have felt: she was forced to go to bed with a man who didn't even want her, having to answer to "Rachel" all night long and pretend to be her pretty sister, knowing that in the morning it was going to be awful. It must have been a soul-destroying experience for both of them. Laban's deceit caused a disaster in Jacob's family life.

Unit 3: Abraham, Isaac and Jacob

OBJECTIVES

Feel...

- shock and disgust at what Laban did to Leah.
- pity for Leah especially, but also for Rachel and Jacob.
- awe that God's word came to pass in spite of all that Laban did to Jacob.

Understand...

- that God's word came to pass: He blessed Jacob because He said He would, and He cursed Laban because He promised to curse those who cursed Abraham's seed.
- that when we depart from God's plan for the family (as Jacob did when he took more than one wife), the result is a disaster.
- that God can and does redeem people and families who have departed from His plan for the family.
- that Laban continually tried to cheat Jacob and would have stolen everything back from him had God not intervened.
- that Jacob had conducted himself with integrity for the entire time he was with Laban: he did not take anything that didn't belong to him and had been entirely honest, and God had blessed him.

Apply this understanding by...

- evaluating your progress towards sowing peace instead of discord within your own family (see Lesson 3.6) and considering additional ways you can bring harmony to your family.

To make matters worse, Laban *then* offered to let Jacob marry Rachel just as soon as the week-long wedding festivities were up (Gen 29:27). So Leah was married to Jacob all of a week before Rachel also joined the household. Leah had no real chance to bond with her husband, and then there was a rival wife, and the wife Jacob really wanted, to boot. Leah was in domestic hell. Meanwhile, Rachel was not in a comfortable position either, suddenly thrown into being a rival wife to her sister, a position she never wanted to be in—and Jacob was caught between them.

God saw this domestic disaster and took pity on Leah (Gen 29:31). Notice that Leah kept hoping that each successive child would cause Jacob to love her, until finally, with Judah, she simply praised God (Gen 29:35). Unfortunately, as Genesis 30:20 shows, Leah didn't stay in that frame of mind; she continued to hope that by giving him more children, Jacob would honor her.

A quick reading of Genesis 29:31-30:24 makes it appear that the events recorded here took place sequentially. They didn't; there wasn't enough time. Only seven years passed between Jacob and Rachel's wedding and the birth of Joseph (Gen 30:25), so the way we should understand the events of this passage is roughly as follows: while Leah was bearing her first four sons, Rachel realized she was barren and gave Bilhah to Jacob. After the birth of Judah, Leah realized that she had stopped bearing and gave her maid Zilpah to Jacob. Zilpah had two children, and then Leah had two more. Somewhere in there, probably a bit after the birth of Judah, Rachel finally had a child of her own, Joseph, around the seven-year mark.

Before Judah and Joseph were born, we have the little incident in Genesis 30:14-16, which gives us a glimpse of the family's home life. Leah and

Jacob's Journey to Haran and Back

1. Jacob set out in haste from Beersheba and camped at Bethel (formerly Luz) before continuing on to Paddan-aram (Gen 28:10-29:1).

2. Jacob served in Laban's house for 20 years before fleeing back to Canaan (Gen 31:1-21).

3. Laban caught up with Jacob in the hill country of Gilead. Then Jacob came to Peniel where he wrestled with God (Gen 31:22-32:31).

4. Esau came up from Seir and met Jacob in peace; Jacob then continued on as far as Shechem (Gen 33).

Unit 3: Abraham, Isaac and Jacob

Rachel were bitter toward each other, and Jacob was caught in the middle. The popular illusion about polygamy imagines a lucky man who gets to have sex indiscriminately with multiple women, and it's okay, because he's married to them all. This is not true; people only think so because our society has been Christian so long that we've lost all cultural memory of what polygamy is *actually* like. In real life, as this text shows us, the wives are always in competition, and the number of children they bear is one of the chief ways they keep score. Frequent intercourse is the key to conception, so a man with multiple wives doesn't sleep with whomever one he wants, whenever he wants—he doesn't dare. The man winds up keeping a schedule in order not to upset the balance of power between his wives. And so we see Jacob forced to stand at stud for Leah because she bought him from Rachel with her mandrakes.

At the seven-year mark, Jacob tried to leave with his family to make his own fortune, but Laban persuaded him to stay, because God was blessing Laban for Jacob's sake (Gen 30:27). They agreed on wages for Jacob, so he could begin to build his own wealth for his family, and Jacob remained with Laban for six more years (Gen 31:38 shows Jacob was with Laban 20 years total, and the first 14 he had no wages, because he was earning his wives; see Gen 31:41). During that six-year period, Laban changed Jacob's wages ten times (Gen 31:7, 41), trying to cheat him, but God kept making Jacob richer at Laban's expense. It appears that Jacob may also have done some manipulation of some sort (Gen 30:37-43) to help the results along.

It is worth comparing this period of Jacob's life with Isaac's growth while he lived with Abimelech. Isaac became mightier than Abimelech, but not at Abimelech's expense, because Abimelech treated him well. Laban treated Jacob poorly, and it cost him, because of the promise God had made to Abraham, which Jacob had inherited: "I will bless those who bless you, and I will curse him who curses you" (Gen 12:3). Laban tried to be a curse to Jacob, and so became cursed himself. Consider the continuity of the Abrahamic promise; it is an important element for understanding Israel's history.

In any case, God had promised to make Jacob great, and He did. Jacob became very rich, and Laban and his sons became very jealous of Jacob (Gen 31:1-2). God told Jacob to leave Laban, and when Jacob conferred with his wives, notice their response in Genesis 31:14-16. Laban had entirely lost the love and respect of his two daughters (and they had a point: he *did* sell them).

So, with his wives on board, Jacob and his family left Laban when he was away shearing his sheep (Gen 31:17-21). They took all the property and livestock that Jacob had acquired while he was with Laban. In addition to their own property, Rachel stole some household gods from her father.

Rachel didn't simply take these idols to make a few extra bucks off her father. Idols in that culture were often attached to a particular piece of property and functioned as a title deed to its plot of land. So Jacob's family was leaving Padan Aram for Canaan, but Rachel was taking with her the deeds to the family land in Padan Aram, just in case.

When Laban pursued and finally caught up with Jacob and his family, he asked, "If you're leaving because you're homesick, why did you take the deeds to the land *here*?" (Gen 31:30*). Rightly or wrongly, Laban's daughters felt that he had

cheated them as well (Gen 31:14-16), and Rachel was trying (wrongly) to even things up.

It's a testament to Jacob's good character and scrupulousness that he could say what he did in Genesis 31:37-39. In spite of constantly changing wages and all the ensuing confusion, Laban couldn't even manage to make a credible accusation that Jacob had taken something of his.

Laban's face-saving response in Genesis 31:43 is very revealing. Even when God had warned him, and he knew he wasn't going to do anything, he still felt himself entitled to everything Jacob had. Jacob was certainly right in Genesis 31:42 that Laban would have kept it all for himself, given the chance. Was any of what Laban saw *actually* his? No; the animals were Jacob's wages, which he had earned; Rachel and Leah were Jacob's wives, for whom he had worked seven years each; the children were his children. *None* of it was Laban's.

At Bethel twenty years earlier, God had promised Jacob, then a poor refugee, to make him great and bring him safely back (Gen 28:13-15). God kept His word, and so He protected Jacob from Laban, and they made a covenant (Gen 31:45-55). The two men were not friends, but they agreed to stay away from one another.

APPLICATION

There is an important negative application to draw from this lesson. Laban, in his greed, alienated his daughters and son-in-law. There is not a lot in life that is more valuable than the people closest to us, but our wicked desire for wealth or happiness or whatever, can so easily rob us of the things that actually make us wealthy. Are there sinful desires that are putting strain on the most valuable relationships in your life? What do you need to do to make it right?

ACTIVITIES

1. Personal Reflection. Reflect on the story by answering the following questions.

What do you think Jacob should have done when he discovered that he had married Leah instead of Rachel?

Lesson 3.7

What are a couple possible ways the story could have turned out differently if Jacob (and maybe even Laban!) had acted according to God's will? _____

_____
_____
_____
_____

2. Journal Time: My Alternate History II. In Lesson 3.6, you had the opportunity to consider how a recent family conflict could have turned out differently if you had acted differently. You were also challenged to consider what you could do to work towards peace in your family. In this journal activity, reflect on how you have been doing at working towards family peace. Consider if you have been doing things to cause conflict between other family members (like Laban did). Answer the following questions.

How have you been doing at making peace in your family? _____

_____
_____
_____
_____
_____
_____
_____

What have you been doing differently in your family relationships to bring about peace? _____

_____
_____
_____
_____
_____
_____
_____

Unit 3: Abraham, Isaac and Jacob

What lessons have you learned about making peace in your family? _____
_____
_____
_____
_____

By giving Rachel and Leah to the same man as wives, Laban set them up for constant conflict. Do you do things that cause conflicts between other people in your family? _____
_____
_____
_____
_____

How can you help make peace in those relationships? _____
_____
_____
_____
_____

What should you do? _____
_____
_____
_____
_____
_____

Lesson 3.7

EVALUATION

1. How was Laban dishonest with Jacob? _____
_____
_____
_____

2. Why did all Laban's attempts to cheat Jacob fail? _____
_____
_____

3. Why did Jacob leave Laban? _____
_____
_____
_____
_____

4. Why did Laban pursue Jacob? _____
_____
_____
_____
_____

UNIT 4: JACOB'S FAMILY

Provoked by the rape of their sister, Jacob's sons broke covenant with a neighboring village and murdered its inhabitants, inciting the peoples of the land against Jacob's household. God protected Jacob's sons and led them back to Bethel where He had first promised to protect and bless Jacob. At Bethel, God repeated His oath to Jacob's sons, but they did not fear God, and after Rachel's death, Jacob was left trying to manage his dangerous offspring. Unlike his older brothers, Joseph had proven himself to be faithful and honest, so Jacob gave him a tunic of authority, but Joseph's brothers resented it and plotted to kill him, eventually selling him into slavery instead. They lied to their father and said Joseph was killed by a wild animal.

Joseph and Judah both departed from their family and came of age in foreign lands. Judah married a Canaanite and had three sons. Two were wicked, and their lives were taken by the Lord. Tamar had married both of Judah's first two sons and Judah had promised her his third, but reneged on his promise. In time, Tamar posed as a prostitute and slept with Judah. When Judah heard that she was pregnant, he was going to have her killed, but she proved that he was the father. She gave birth to twins, one of whom was the next in the seed-line. Meanwhile, Joseph came of age as a slave in Egypt, but he was faithful to the Lord and became head of his master's house. Falsely accused of attempted rape by his master's wife, he was imprisoned and became head of the prison. In time, he interpreted Pharaoh's dream and was promoted to head over all Egypt, second only to Pharaoh.

When God brought a region-wide famine, Egypt was prepared because Joseph had been able to interpret Pharaoh's dream, but Canaan was not prepared. Jacob's family ran out of food, so he sent his sons to Egypt to buy grain. When they arrived in Egypt, Joseph (whom they didn't recognize) met with them. Joseph immediately saw and joined in with what God was doing. Through a series of tests, God (using Joseph) transformed the brothers from people who would kill or sell their own brother to people who would die in the place of their brother. They were restored to Joseph and reconciled to their father, and the entire family moved to the finest land in Egypt.

Jacob moved to Egypt, believing that God would raise the nation there and bring them back home to the promised land. While in Egypt, Jacob grew old and transferred his covenant blessings to his sons. Judah received the blessing of rulership, and Joseph received the double inheritance of the firstborn; the other sons each received a prophetic blessing. Jacob and Joseph both died in Egypt, instructing their family to bury them in Canaan because they trusted in God's promise to return the nation there.

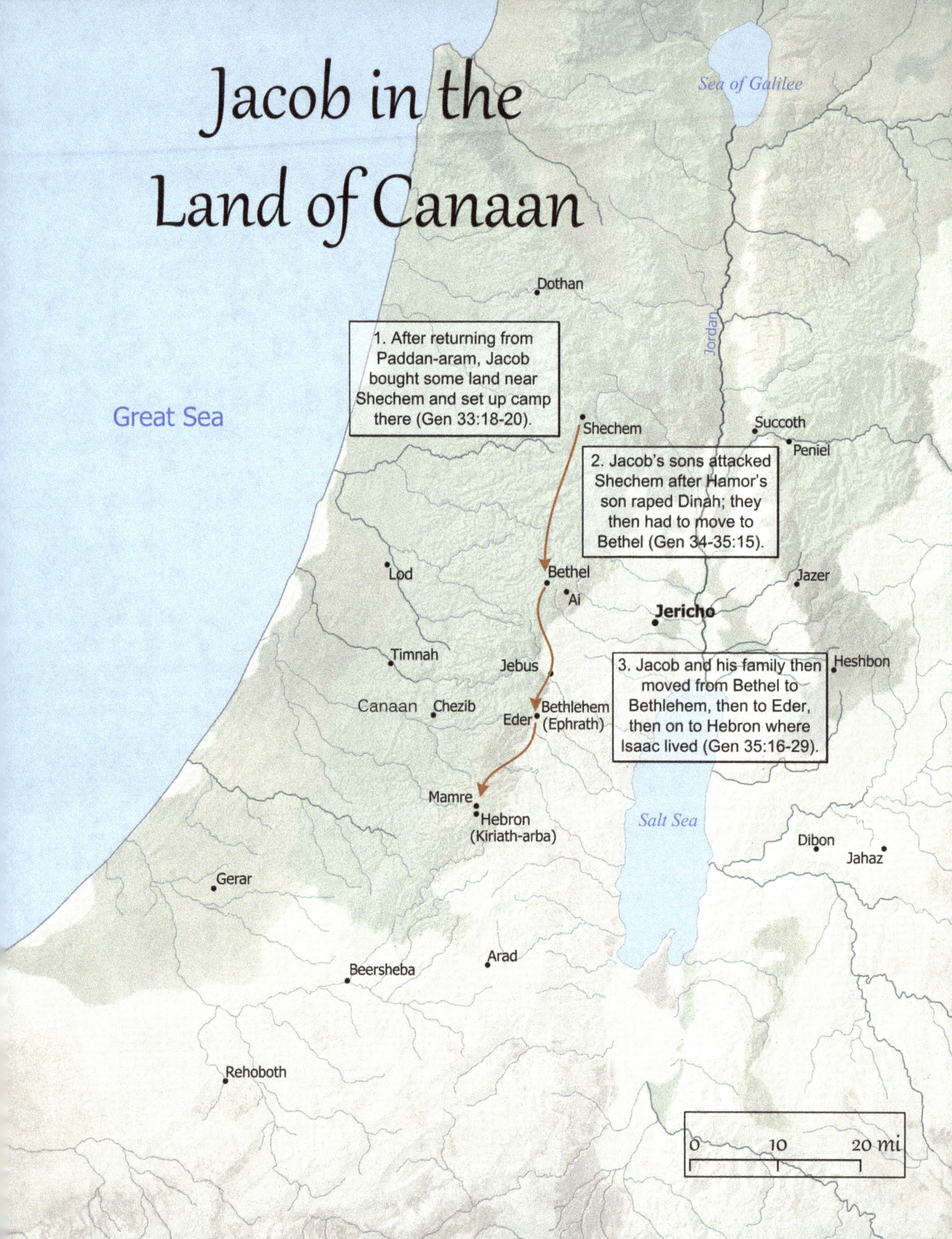

LESSON 4.1

Jacob's Family in the Land

UNIT 4

STORY

Lesson Theme - God protected Jacob's family in spite of their wickedness.

Jacob's sons were totally out of control; instead of being a blessing to all the families of the earth as God had intended, they had become a curse to them. However, God was still protecting Jacob and his family as He had promised, and He was making Jacob into a great power in the land that He had promised to Abraham and his family.

Genesis 34 records a strange incident. Shechem, a Hittite from the neighboring village by the same name, raped Dinah, a daughter of Jacob and full sister of Simeon and Levi. As a result, Shechem fell deeply in love with her and sought permission from Jacob's family to marry her (Gen 34:1-4).

The idea that a rapist could love his victim or that he would dare to think of marrying her falls strangely on 21st-century ears. There are a few important details that help us make sense of this. (1) In many pagan societies throughout history, and even today, women have been regarded as property. (2) Shechem's desire to possess Dinah was sincere. Of course, it did not rise to the biblical requirements of love—he *raped* her, after all—but he really did want her for his wife, and within his society, what he did was *common*. Take this story as an opportunity to cultivate gratitude that you've been born into a Christian society where such things are unthinkable. (3) On the matter of a girl marrying her rapist, Dinah had very few options. In the societies of the

OVERVIEW

After one of their neighbors raped their sister Dinah, Jacob's sons made and murderously broke a covenant with a nearby village, provoking the peoples of the land to destroy Jacob's household. God protected Jacob's sons and led them back to Bethel where He had first promised to protect and bless Jacob. At Bethel, God repeated His oath to Jacob's sons. Rachel and Isaac died, and Jacob was left trying to manage his dangerous offspring.

SOURCE MATERIAL

- Genesis 34-35
- Psalm 104
- Proverbs 14:16-17

time, it was assumed that a woman was a virgin at marriage, and a woman who was not a virgin would likely have *no* opportunity to marry. None. Strange as it may seem to us, nobody would want her—and this was true whether she gave away her virginity willingly or it was taken from her by a rapist. Staying single was not an attractive option, because there were few ways for a woman alone to make a living, especially as she got older. Everything was physical work. The only viable retirement plan was having lots of kids who could take care of her when she was older—for which she would need a husband. The one man who could not possibly complain that she wasn't a virgin was the man who was responsible

Unit 4: Jacob's Family

OBJECTIVES

Feel...

- gratitude to be living in a Christian society where rape is considered a serious crime rather than a relatively ordinary way of getting a wife.
- gratitude to be living in a Christian society where women have the freedom to earn a living without having to be completely dependent on a husband and children for their livelihood.
- disgust at Jacob's sons for perverting the sign of the covenant and murdering their own family members.

Understand...

- that although the rape of Dinah was certainly a sin, it was a relatively common occurrence in that society, and it greatly constricted Dinah's options for her future.
- that marrying Shechem was almost certainly Dinah's *only* good option for a safe and secure future in her old age.
- that circumcision was a really *big* deal because it made the entire village of Shechem into children of Abraham.
- that God had fulfilled His promises to Jacob and made him *very* wealthy.
- that Jacob's family was becoming like the other peoples in the land.

Apply this understanding by...

- considering how your own anger causes you to be foolish.
- praising God for the wealth He has given to us.

for that fact—her rapist. So as rotten a situation as it was, Dinah's best prospect for long-term well-being was to marry Shechem. (This, by the way, is why the Law of Moses *requires* marriage in exactly this situation, unless the girl's family absolutely forbids it.)

Jacob was obviously considering a harsh response to Hamor and Shechem, because he waited for his sons to come in from the field before giving an answer (Gen 34:5). Once upon a time, Jacob was a force to be reckoned with in his own right (remember that he wrestled with an angel *all night*, and anybody who has done any wrestling knows even a few minutes can be very draining), but that was before he got his hip dislocated. These days, he wasn't much of a fighter, and so he waited for his sons.

However, when his sons came, they didn't give the harsh response that Jacob expected. Notice that "the sons of Jacob...spoke deceitfully" (Gen 34:13). Simeon and Levi would do most of the dirty work, but all the boys were in on it. (Joseph may not have been involved, given what we know of his character, but the rest of the brothers probably were.)

The condition of Dinah's marriage was that all the males of the village had to become circumcised (Gen 34:15). Don't miss the significance of this. Circumcision was the mark of the covenant God had made with Abraham. Being circumcised meant *becoming a member of Abraham's family*. The entire village of Shechem *joined the covenant family and became part of the seed of Abraham*. Simeon and Levi abused the sign of the covenant in order to gain a tactical advantage.

Shechem was eager to marry Dinah and didn't delay in getting circumcised (Gen 34:19). Then he returned to his city and urged them to get circumcised in order to receive all the benefits of being in covenant with Jacob's family (a bigger pool of people for marriage as well as economic benefits—Gen 34:23). They all consented and all the males in Shechem were circumcised (Gen 34:24).

As a result, the men of the city were weak while they recovered from their circumcision... and, of course, that was the point. While they were recovering, Simeon and Levi came into the city and killed all the males (Gen 34:25-26). Because Simeon and Levi abused circumcision to weaken the men of Shechem, *they were killing members of their own family, God's chosen people*. When the rest of Jacob's sons came upon the city, plundered it, and enslaved the women and children (Gen 34:28-29), *they were stealing from and enslaving their own family*, and they thought nothing of it.

Jacob objected to his sons' behavior, but not based on moral principle, but rather on expediency. He took the rape seriously and intended to deal harshly with it—which is why he waited for his sons to come home before he gave Hamor an answer. Jacob didn't want Shechem to get away with raping Dinah. But the *way* his sons went about seeking revenge on Shechem was a diplomatic disaster. By making a covenant with Hamor *and then breaking it*, they made themselves untrustworthy. If the people of the land could not trust Jacob's family to keep their word, then having Jacob's family for neighbors was just too dangerous, and everybody would be better off banding together and killing Jacob's whole family (Gen 34:30). In fact, this would have happened except that God prevented it (Gen 35:5). So Jacob's objection was that they weren't going to be able to live there anymore, because nobody could trust them. Jacob's sons weren't wise enough to see his point; they were just mad about how Dinah had been treated.

God took all of Jacob's family back to Bethel so that Jacob could worship and fulfill his vows (Gen 35:1). However, notice that God's timing also moved the whole clan away from the site of the recent bloodshed. God called His people back to worship after their sin.

This call back to Bethel was also a signal that God had fulfilled all that He had promised to Jacob. He had made him great, multiplied his possessions and family, and kept them all safe in the land. Jacob was very, very wealthy, but his wealth won't remain (he was very diminished by the time he went down into Egypt).

Jacob had to tell everyone to put away foreign gods from among them (Gen 35:2). This should not have been necessary to start with, and it indicates that there was a lot of idolatry in Jacob's house. Rachel would have had to bury Laban's household gods, but as we will see later in Judah's story, their idolatry problem was much, much more widespread than that. The point here is that Jacob's family was slowly acclimating to the people of the land; they were becoming like their neighbors.

The death of Isaac was the end of his testimony and presence in the land (Gen 35:29). Now the family of Jacob was carrying the torch, and it is increasingly obvious that they were not up to the task.

Unit 4: Jacob's Family

APPLICATION

Jacob's sons were angry, and in their anger, they were blind. Some sort of retribution might have been necessary, but that was in God's hands. Instead, Simeon and Levi, in anger, took revenge in their own wicked manner. Not only were their actions morally wrong, they were just plain foolish. Their deception and murder of the people of Shechem ruined their reputation among the people of the land and might have gotten them killed, had God not protected them.

This is how anger always works. Proverbs 14:16-17 is a meditation on the folly of getting carried away by one's own anger. Anger leads to folly. Jacob's sons exemplified these proverbs in spades, and they didn't even realize they had made a mistake afterwards, which is the way fools work. Is there anger in your life that is causing folly that you are not even aware of? Ask God to reveal anything that you need to repent of, and in His grace, He will; *and* He will give you the power to change.

ACTIVITIES

1. Anger Management. Make a list of the last five times you were angry. Write down at least one lesson you can learn from one of those situations. If you can't think of anything, ask for help. Don't be like Jacob's sons—actually listen to the counsel you get. Write your reflections in the space below.

2. Thanksgiving. Imagine what life would be like if you lived in a tent like Jacob. Then make a list below of all of things you would miss that you presently enjoy in your life (air-conditioning, etc).

_____
_____
_____
_____
_____
_____
_____
_____

In many ways, you are more wealthy than Jacob was, even though he was a king. Write a short prayer thanking the Lord for all of the wealth that He has given you. _____

_____
_____
_____
_____
_____
_____
_____
_____
_____
_____
_____

Unit 4: Jacob's Family

3. Read Psalm 104. Then, in the space below write a psalm of your own, modeled after Psalm 104, thanking God for all He has done for you.

Lesson 4.1

EVALUATION

1. What would Dinah's life have been like as a rape victim in that society? _____
_____
_____

2. Evaluate Shechem's offer to marry Dinah. Was this a good thing or a bad thing? _____
_____
_____

3. What was the significance of the circumcision covenant with the village of Shechem? _____
_____
_____

4. So what were Simeon and Levi doing when they killed all the newly circumcised men in Shechem?
_____
_____

5. What was Jacob's objection to his sons' act? Was he right? _____
_____
_____

6. Why did God call Jacob back to Bethel? _____
_____
_____

7. What is the significance of the death of Isaac? _____
_____
_____

8. Was Jacob's family up to the challenge? Why or why not? _____
_____
_____
_____

LESSON 4.2

Joseph's Dreams and Betrayal by His Brothers

UNIT 4

STORY

Lesson Theme - The fall of Jacob's sons
Jacob's sons committed both the sin of Adam, father-hatred, and the sin of Cain, brother-murder (symbolically). Jacob "died" when he heard about Joseph's "death." The next several lessons are about the redemption of Joseph's brothers (especially Judah), and the "resurrection" of Jacob when he was restored to Joseph.

Joseph was favored by his father because "he was the son of his old age" (Gen 37:3). The Sunday school version of this story is told as though Joseph were a 12-year-old and his brothers were all 25 or 30. Daddy was playing favorites, the story goes, and always gave Joseph better presents at Christmas. This version of the story is certainly not the right narrative.

Actually, Judah and Joseph were right about the same age. We know this because Joseph was born the seventh year after Jacob married Leah and Rachel (Gen 30:25), and Judah was Leah's fourth son (after Reuben, Simeon and Levi); so assuming Leah bore a son every one and a half to two years means Judah and Joseph were born in about the same year. Zilpah's sons and Leah's later sons were all younger than Joseph (Gad, Issachar, Asher and Zebulun).

Jacob's favor for Joseph was covenantal, not primarily emotional. The tunic Jacob gave to Joseph represented the authority and blessing of firstborn status. Of course, Joseph wasn't firstborn, but because of his older brothers' failures, he had been elevated to that status.

OVERVIEW

Joseph's older brothers had forfeited the blessing of Jacob's covenantal favor, so it was passed to Joseph who had proven himself to be faithful and honest. His father gave him a tunic of authority representing this favor, but Joseph's brothers resented him for it and plotted to kill him. Reuben talked his brothers into throwing Joseph into a pit so he could save him later. However, after Reuben was gone, Judah convinced his brothers to sell Joseph into slavery. They lied to their father and said that Joseph was killed by a wild animal, and his father experienced the loss as a death-like experience.

SOURCE MATERIAL

- Genesis 37
- Psalm 28
- Proverbs 17:17, 18:19

Reuben lost his father's favor when he slept with his father's concubine Bilhah (see Gen 35:22) (probably in an attempt to supplant his father). Simeon and Levi lost their father's favor when they cruelly attacked and killed all the men of Shechem (see Gen 34). Therefore, either Joseph or Judah was the next in line for the blessing of being firstborn. And even if Judah was slightly older, Joseph had probably proven himself to be trustworthy, upright and faithful.

Unit 4: Jacob's Family

OBJECTIVES

Feel...

- grateful for Jacob's wisdom in honoring Joseph with the covenantal blessing.
- sadness for the brothers' hatred of Joseph.
- a sense of loss at the brothers' fall in plotting to kill Joseph.

Understand...

- the nature of Joseph's covenantal blessing.
- what Joseph's tunic represented.
- the age relationship between Joseph and his brothers, especially Judah.
- that the brothers' plot to kill Joseph was in keeping with their normal pattern of behavior.
- which brothers showed kindness to Joseph in the plot to kill him.
- the nature of the brothers' sin against their father.
- how Jacob responded when he heard about Joseph's death.

Apply this understanding by...

- evaluating your relationship with your brothers and sisters to determine whether you are more like Joseph, Reuben, Judah, or the rest of the brothers.
- confessing any sin of betrayal against a brother, sister or friend and working towards restoration.

Joseph is referred to as the "son of [Jacob's] old age" (Gen 37:3), because he was the miraculously conceived son of Jacob's chosen wife and the only son of Rachel at this time (Benjamin was born later). Joseph was a special gift to Jacob, and God's favor was upon him. Jacob recognized God's hand of blessing on Joseph and reflected this understanding in his treatment of Joseph.

It is not surprising then, that Joseph's brothers hated him; he was receiving the favor of their father that a number of them had forfeited. To add insult to injury, he had brought a bad report of his brothers to their father (Gen 37:2) *and* was having dreams of his own greatness (in the first dream his brothers bowed down to him, and in the second even his father and mother bowed) and telling them about it (Gen 37:5-11)! Even though the dreams were prophetic, Joseph certainly came across to his brothers as self-righteous and arrogant; but mostly, his brothers were just resentful because Joseph had supplanted them due to their failures.

The sons of Jacob had a history of set-up and ambush. They did it first to Hamor, Shechem and the men of their city. They spoke deceitfully to them to make them vulnerable (they talked them into circumcising themselves—Gen 34:13). Then, when the men of Shechem were recovering from their circumcision, Simeon and Levi came and killed all the men of the city, and the rest of the brothers joined them to plunder the slain.

So when the brothers saw Joseph from a distance and started plotting their ambush (Gen 37:18), they were acting completely in character. They were spies; they spied out their enemies and sought to get them in a vulnerable position so that they could kill them. Joseph, as the object of their hatred, was on the receiving end of this treatment.

Reuben was the one brother who retained his dignity in this act. He convinced his brothers to throw Joseph into a pit instead of shedding his

blood, so he could come back and save him later (Gen 37:21-22). Reuben was gone when Judah (unaware of Reuben's plan to come back and save him) came up with the plan to sell Joseph so they wouldn't be responsible for his blood. Throughout the Joseph narrative, slavery is a symbolic equivalent to death, and as far as Joseph's brothers were concerned, when they sold him into slavery, Joseph was as good as dead. They didn't expect to ever see him again.

The brothers' final act of sin in this story was against their father. They had sold his favored son into slavery, and now they lied to him to cover it up. Jacob responded by saying that he would "go down into the grave to [his] son in mourning" (Gen 37:35). Throughout the rest of the Joseph narrative, Jacob speaks as though his life was bound up with Joseph's and later, with Benjamin's. Losing Joseph was a death-like experience for Jacob, and the story anticipates a resurrection experience upon Joseph's restoration.

APPLICATION

The story of Jacob's sons has several lessons about family dynamics and relationships between siblings and parents. The lives of Jacob and his sons were much more difficult than they needed to be. The relationships were filled with spite, revenge and betrayal—this stuff could have been avoided with a little relational sense and grace—gifts that God is happy to give to those who ask.

How is your relationship with your siblings and parents? Are there any areas in which you need to repent? Are there character issues behind your behaviors that are causing problems (perhaps envy or shame)? God loves to heal those who come to Him for help; bring your problems before the Lord, and see what He does.

ACTIVITIES

1. Draw It: Joseph's Dreams. In the space below, draw what Joseph saw in his two dreams. Then answer the questions below.

(1) Draw eleven sheaves representing Joseph's eleven brothers bowing down to his sheaf.

Unit 4: Jacob's Family

(2) Draw eleven stars representing Joseph's eleven brothers as well as the sun and moon representing his mother and father bowing down to him.

Why were sheaves chosen to represent the brothers? _____
_____

Why do stars represent the brothers and the sun and moon represent Joseph's parents in the second dream? _____
_____

Did Jacob believe Joseph's dreams or not? _____

Why did Jacob rebuke Joseph if he believed him?_____
_____

2. Psalm 28. Psalm 28 sounds like a prayer Joseph might have prayed while stuck in the pit. Read this psalm and write a short response._____
_____
_____
_____
_____
_____

3. Journal Time: Which Brother Are You? In the story of Joseph's brothers selling him into slavery, most of his brothers were jealous and spiteful toward him, but both Reuben and Judah tried to help Joseph. Spend some time writing in the space below, thinking about your own family life. Are you more like Reuben, Judah, or the rest of the brothers? Or are you maybe like Joseph? Are there any areas in your relationship with your parents or siblings where you need to repent? _____

_____
_____
_____
_____
_____

EVALUATION

1. What was Joseph's age in relation to the rest of his brothers? _____
_____

2. Why did Joseph get the covenantal blessing from Jacob if he wasn't firstborn? _____
_____

3. What did the tunic that Jacob gave Joseph represent? _____
_____

4. Why did the brothers want to kill Joseph? _____
_____

5. Is it surprising that Joseph's brothers were willing to go to the extreme of killing him in their hatred? _____
_____

6. Which brothers tried to help Joseph? _____
_____
_____

7. How did Jacob receive the news of Joseph's "death"? _____
_____

LESSON 4.3

Joseph and Judah Came of Age in Foreign Lands

UNIT 4

STORY

Lesson Theme - Joseph was faithful and was exalted; Judah was wicked, but repented.

This lesson compares and contrasts Joseph's and Judah's coming of age experiences. Joseph and Judah were about the same age and followed similar paths to maturity, only Judah took the low road, and Joseph took the high road. Joseph went against his will into Egypt, suffered until the Lord exalted him, and was faithful to God throughout. Judah went willingly to the Canaanites and made allegiances with them, turning from his God. As a result, his wicked sons were killed, and his Canaanite daughter-in-law led him to repentance. Judah's repentance in this lesson is a *big deal.* Judah, continued the seed-line, not Joseph (as we might expect). Judah disdained his seed but was called to repentance by his Canaanite/prostitute daughter-in-law. God likes to redeem a real mess!

Judah's coming of age

Befriending and marrying a Canaanite as Judah did was not okay. First, Noah spoke a curse against the Canaanites (Gen 9:25), then both Isaac and Jacob were not to marry among the Canaanites, so they both married women from their homeland. Judah should have followed the same precedent.

Now, it is not *always* wrong for an Israelite to marry a Canaanite (or Egyptian as the case may be). It is perfectly acceptable for sons of Israel to marry Canaanites so long as they convert to Yahweh-worship first. But that was not what was going on with Judah; he had departed from

OVERVIEW

Joseph and Judah both departed from their family and came of age in foreign lands, Joseph unwillingly and Judah willingly. Judah married a Canaanite and had children with her (something he should not have done). Two of his sons were wicked, and their lives were taken by the Lord. Tamar had married both of Judah's first two sons and was going to marry his third, but Judah wrongfully prevented this. In time, Tamar posed as a prostitute under-veil and slept with Judah. When Judah heard that she was pregnant, he was going to have her killed, but she proved that *he* had slept with her. One of her sons became the next in the seed-line. Joseph came of age in Egypt against his will, but he was faithful to the Lord and was blessed. His master's wife tried to seduce him and he fled, leading to his wrongful imprisonment. Joseph became ruler over the prison, and in time, he was taken before Pharaoh to interpret Pharaoh's dream. Joseph then became second only to Pharaoh over all of Egypt.

SOURCE MATERIAL

- Genesis 38-41
- Psalm 88
- Proverbs 28:20

his family and from his faith as well. He was not out evangelizing the Canaanites—they were not joining him; he was joining them. There is a big difference.

Unit 4: Jacob's Family

OBJECTIVES

Feel...

- shock at Judah's willingness to abandon his family and heritage and ally himself with Canaanites so easily.
- surprise and disgust that Judah would sleep with a shrine prostitute.
- gratitude to God for redeeming Judah's messed up situation and providing a seed through him.
- awe at Joseph's purity and faithfulness in Egypt.

Understand...

- why Judah was wrong in departing from his family and marrying a Canaanite.
- that Tamar was wrong in seducing her father-in-law as a prostitute, but that God used it to bring Judah to repentance for His glory.
- that Tamar's seduction of Judah produced the next descendant of the seed-line, showing that God likes to use messed up situations for His glory.
- that Joseph's faithfulness led to him ruling over all of Egypt.

Apply this understanding by...

- identifying a situation in your life where you are rebelling like Judah and then choosing to repent from your rebellion like Judah did.
- identifying a situation in your life where you can be faithful like Joseph was even when your life is out of his control.

In time, Judah had sons by his Canaanite wife, the daughter of Shua. Judah found a wife, Tamar, for his firstborn son, Er. But God took Er's life because "he was wicked in the sight of the LORD" (Gen 38:7). According to the customs of the time, Judah's second son, Onan, was to marry Tamar, and his first child by Tamar would have been reckoned as Er's son. However, Onan didn't want to honor his brother, so he emitted on the ground, for which God took his life too (Gen 38:8-10). By now, Judah was beginning to notice a pattern: whoever married Tamar ended up dead, and Judah didn't want his only remaining son to die too. (Of course, Judah was wrong to think Tamar was at fault for his sons' deaths. If anything, it was Judah's fault for raising wicked sons in a wicked land.) Judah had no intention of giving Tamar to his youngest son, Shelah, so he lied to her and told her to be a widow until Shelah was old enough to marry (Gen 38:11).

In time, Tamar got the hint. So she dressed up like a *sacred* prostitute to trick Judah himself into sleeping with her (this is where Judah really abandoned his faith). It worked (surprise, surprise); Judah slept with Tamar without knowing whom he had slept with (Gen 38:13-19). When Judah heard that Tamar was pregnant, he was prepared to put her to death, until she proved that it was he who had slept with her (Gen 38:24-26).

Here the story takes a surprising turn. Considering that Judah was caught red-handed in his sin, it's not surprising that he felt badly about wanting to kill Tamar and repented. What is surprising is that Tamar turns out to be the *heroine* of the story *for* prostituting herself to Judah so as to reveal his sin and bring him to repentance. The outcome of Judah's repentance did not make Tamar's prostitution somehow acceptable; but clearly, Tamar was more righteous than Judah

(Gen 38:26). Her son is in the seed-line, and her name is mentioned in Matthew's genealogy (Matt 1:3). (As a contrast, notice that Judah's wife is never even named in this story.) God takes backwards, broken, messed up people and situations and turns them for His glory.

Joseph's coming of age
Joseph ended up in a foreign land, not unlike Judah. However, while he was in Egypt against his will, he still remained faithful to God. Everywhere Joseph went, God blessed him. He became the head servant in Potiphar's house (Gen 39:4). When Potiphar's wife tried to seduce him, he fled (Gen 39:12). Joseph fled from sexual immorality—a big contrast to Judah, who married a Canaanite and slept with a prostitute. Joseph was falsely accused of sin and ended up in prison (Gen 39:20), while Judah was rightly accused of sin (the redeeming part for Judah being that he actually repented).

While in prison, Joseph's faithfulness again brought blessing. He became the ruler (of sorts) over the entire prison (Gen 39:22). When Joseph had the opportunity to interpret the dreams of the baker and butler, God blessed his efforts (Gen 40). Joseph's hopes of getting out of prison were delayed for two more years, but he finally got a chance to interpret Pharaoh's dreams (Gen 41). Pharaoh was so impressed with Joseph's discernment and wisdom that he made him second in command over all of Egypt (Gen 41:40).

During all of these ups and downs, Joseph did not give up on God and start worshiping the gods of the Egyptians. In fact, the opposite is true; Joseph was busy converting the people of Egypt to Yahweh worship (this will become clear when Joseph's brothers come to Egypt in the next lesson).

Comparing Joseph and Judah
Judah and Joseph both came of age in a foreign land; but while Judah gave himself over to the Canaanites, Joseph turned the Egyptians to worship Yahweh. Judah took what he wanted (Tamar), while Joseph ran from the seductress. But Judah's story is not all bad; he did repent, and he bore the seed-line to the next generation.

Joseph and Judah both provide good models of behavior, depending on where we are in life. Joseph had no control over his life; he was *forced* to go to Egypt, *forced* to work for Potiphar and *forced* to go to prison. Many of life's decisions are made for us and are outside of our control; our responsibility is to respond like Joseph and be faithful. Judah was a free man, but he *chose* to rebel in his freedom; he *chose* to leave his home and family and make wicked friends. It is inevitable that we will turn from God (at times) in areas where we are given freedom. When we do, God will reveal our sins to us in time and we should repent like Judah did.

APPLICATION

Joseph was faithful in a foreign land while Judah was unfaithful among the Canaanites. In different ways, their lifestyles caused them hardship. Because of his faithfulness, Joseph was thrown in prison. Because of his unfaithfulness, Judah lost his sons. Here's the deal: life is going to bring about hardships whether you are faithful to the Lord or not. It's better to suffer for righteousness than wickedness.

Lesson 4.3

The good news is that it is never too late to repent. Of course, even when we do repent, that doesn't make the cost of our sins go away; Judah didn't get his sons back when he repented. But the sooner we repent, the better. Is there an area in your life where you are on a path to destruction? Repent and experience forgiveness.

ACTIVITIES

1. Graph It. Joseph's life was full of ups and downs. Draw a graph of Joseph's life with the x-axis being a timeline of his life starting in Canaan when he went to check on his brothers and ending with him in Egypt second in command to Pharaoh. The y-axis goes from the most discouraging low points at the bottom (-5) to the most blessed high points at the top (+5). You can use the graph on the following page, or draw a larger one on a separate piece of paper. The following consecutive events are marked at the bottom of the graph from 1-8: (1) being thrown into the pit by his brothers, (2) taken out of the pit, (3) sold into slavery in Potiphar's house, (4) ruling over Potiphar's house, (5) falsely thrown into prison, (6) ruling over prison, (7) discouragement when the butler did not remember him, (8) ruling over Egypt. Draw a small picture at of each of the 8 events next to where you mark them on the graph.

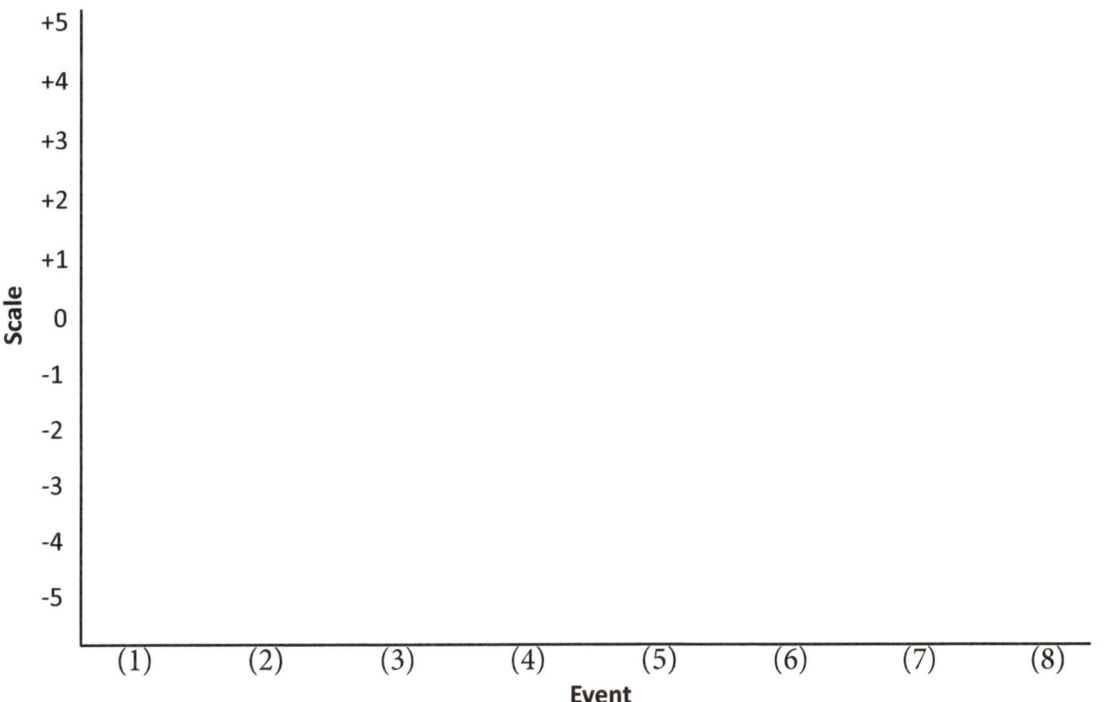

Unit 4: Jacob's Family

2. Personal Reflection. Answer the following questions.

What do you think the lowest point in Joseph's life was? Why? _____

_____
_____
_____
_____
_____
_____

How do you think Joseph felt at his low points and how might he have responded and prayed? _____

_____
_____
_____
_____
_____
_____

Was Joseph's faithfulness to God rewarded? _____

_____
_____
_____
_____
_____
_____

3. Journal Time: Application. Consider the following and write your responses in space below.

Like Joseph, each of us will go through times in our life where our circumstances are outside of our control. It is our duty to be faithful, pray and seek God in those times as Joseph did. Think about a time in your life when you have been in a discouraging situation and couldn't do anything about it. How did you respond? How should you have responded? _____

Unit 4: Jacob's Family

Like Judah, each of us will be given freedom to make decisions, and we will, at times, really mess it up. When God reveals our sin, we are to repent, quickly and fully as Judah did. Think about a time in your life when you made a bad decision and God convicted you of your sin. How did you respond? Did you repent? How should you have responded? _____

_____
_____
_____
_____
_____
_____
_____
_____
_____
_____
_____
_____
_____
_____
_____
_____
_____
_____
_____
_____
_____
_____

Lesson 4.3

EVALUATION

1. Why was it wrong for Judah to depart from his family, reside with the Canaanites and marry a Canaanite? _____
_____
_____
_____

2. Was it ever okay for an Israelite to marry a Canaanite or Egyptian? _____
_____
_____

3. It seems odd that God chose Judah and his son through Tamar to continue the seed-line after Judah's sinful departure from his family. Why do you suppose God did this? _____
_____
_____
_____

4. How many times did Joseph fall into a "pit" and then rise back up? Describe each time. _____
_____
_____
_____
_____
_____
_____
_____

5. Why do you think God blessed Joseph? _____
_____
_____
_____

LESSON 4.4

Joseph's Brothers Tested in Egypt

UNIT 4

THE STORY

Lesson Theme - Jacob's family transformed and reconciled

This lesson is about the reconciliation of Joseph and his brothers and the restoration of his brothers to a proper relationship with their father, Jacob. This reconciliation wasn't just about Joseph forgiving his brothers; he had already done that (see Gen 41:51—God had allowed Joseph to forget his family). Rather, God used Joseph to expose his brothers' sin and bring them to a place of repentance *and* transformation. The leaders of the 12 tribes of the chosen nation *could not* be brother-murderers and father-haters, or we would just have another Babel on our hands. God used Joseph to *change* his brothers, to lead them to a place where they choose to protect their littlest brother out of love for their father.

While in Egypt, God had blessed Joseph and brought him to a position of authority second only to Pharaoh. Joseph had interpreted Pharaoh's two dreams that had both indicated a famine was coming. In order to prepare for the lean years, Joseph gathered grain for seven years that could be distributed in the years of the famine that followed (Gen 41:37-57).

Sure enough, the famine came—and not just to Egypt. All over the region there was a dearth of food. The food was distributed in Egypt and beyond. Even Jacob's family, in Canaan, was acutely experiencing the effects of the famine. It got so bad, that Jacob sent his sons to Egypt to buy some grain that he heard was available there (Gen 43:1-2).

OVERVIEW

God brought a region-wide famine into the land that affected Canaan as well as Egypt. Egypt was prepared for this famine because Joseph had been able to interpret Pharaoh's dream. Jacob's family ran out of food, so he sent his sons to Egypt to buy grain. When they arrived in Egypt, Joseph (whom they didn't recognize) met with them. Joseph immediately saw and joined in with what God was doing. Through a series of tests, God (using Joseph) transformed the brothers from people who would kill or sell their own brother to people who would die in the place of their brother. They were restored to Joseph and reconciled to their father, and the entire family moved to the finest land in Egypt.

SOURCE MATERIAL

- Genesis 42-45
- Proverbs 3:5-6
- Psalm 11

When the brothers arrived in Egypt (all except Benjamin, whom Jacob would not allow to go), they had to appear before Joseph, who was in charge of distributing the grain (Gen 42:6). Joseph immediately recognized them when they bowed down before him (remember Joseph's dream) and sought his favor (Gen 42:7). And immediately, God began to use Joseph to put his brothers through a series of three tests, the first two setting the stage for the final test. In the

Unit 4: Jacob's Family

OBJECTIVES

Feel...

- a sense of God's guidance as sons of Jacob met with their long lost brother in Egypt and went through the "tests."
- thankfulness that the brothers were convicted of their sin as they met with Joseph.
- wonder at how God brought about the transformation of the brothers.

Understand...

- that God was not just interested in forgiveness (Joseph had already forgiven his brothers); God was interested in reconciliation and rebuilding trust.
- how the series of tests Joseph and God put the brothers through brought about their transformation.
- how God used circumstances to direct the lives of Jacob's sons toward transformation.
- that the high point of the story is when Judah offered to be a slave in place of Benjamin.

Apply this understanding by...

- evaluating your life to see how God might be using circumstances to bring about transformation and praying that God would reveal what He is doing in your life.

final test, God, through Joseph, put the brothers in the same kind of situation they were in when they betrayed their father's trust and sold their brother Joseph into slavery. They would either have to betray their father's trust again and sell their youngest brother, Benjamin, into slavery in Egypt, or offer themselves in Benjamin's place.

As we watch the narrative unfold, we can now see how the first two tests were preparatory for the final one.

As soon as the brothers arrived and met with Joseph (they didn't find out that he was Joseph until the very end of the narrative), they were seemingly mistreated. Joseph accused them of coming to spy out the land and find its weaknesses so that they could plunder it (Gen 42:9). Of course, the brothers *were* spies; they spied out Shechem and attacked them when they were weakest. They spied on Joseph as he came to check on them and plotted how they could kill him. But now they denied being spies, even though what Joseph accused them of was completely within character for them. In fact, it is quite possible that the brothers' plan was to meet with the grain keeper to figure out how they could attack at night and steal all the grain they needed.

Joseph's plan was to get Benjamin to Egypt so he could test how they would treat that brother. So Joseph threatened to keep all but one of them in prison until Benjamin came. When he made this threat, the brothers were convicted of their sin against Joseph and believed that they were being punished for how they had treated him (Gen 42:14-24). In the end, Joseph kept only Simeon. And thus the first test: would they return and save their brother or let him rot in Egypt like they did Joseph?

Furthermore, before the brothers left, Joseph told his servants to hide the money the brothers had paid him in their sacks of grain (Gen 42:25), which only served to increase the brothers' fear of returning for Simeon. They knew that if they returned to Egypt, they would, in all likelihood, be accused of stealing—after all, Joseph had already expressed great mistrust in them.

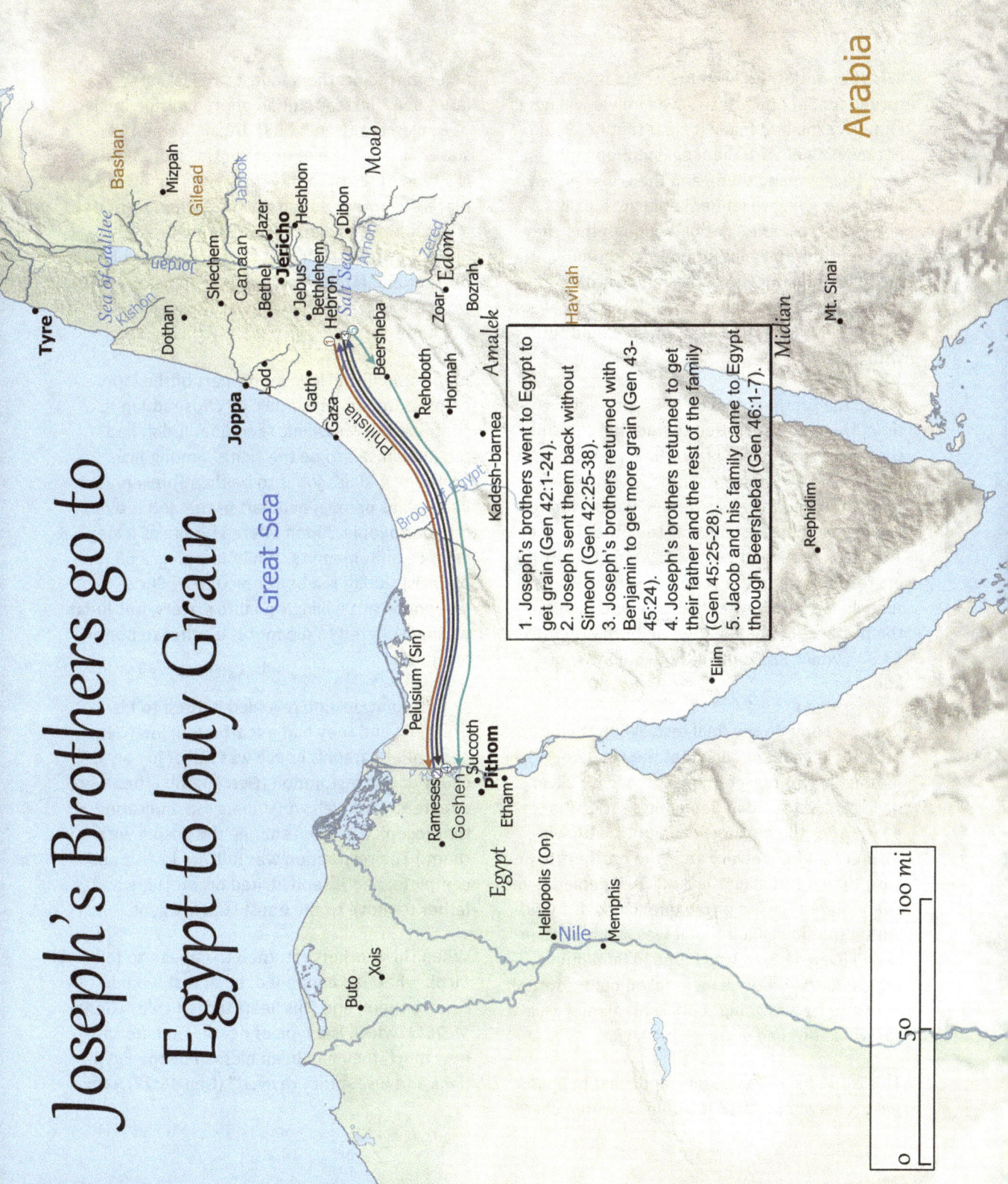

Unit 4: Jacob's Family

Whether or not the brothers would have returned for Simeon *just* to save him we will never know. Joseph had made it clear that he would not even meet with them again if Benjamin didn't accompany them, and there was no way Jacob was going to let Benjamin go. Finally, however, the famine got bad enough that they had to return to Egypt for grain; and reluctantly, Jacob let Benjamin go with them, warning them that his life was wrapped up with the boy's (Gen 43:11-14). If Benjamin died, Jacob would "die" with grief.

When the brothers arrived in Egypt a second time, they were surprised to find that this time they were treated with favor (in fact, they were not sure if it was favor or some kind of a trick). Benjamin especially was treated with favor, receiving five times as much as the other brothers. This was the second test: how would the brothers respond when the youngest was favored like Joseph had been? Joseph also "weirded out" the brothers by seating them in birth order (Gen 43:33), which he would have had no way of knowing.

We now come to the final test. When the brothers left (still not knowing that they had been interacting with Joseph), Joseph had his silver divining cup placed in Benjamin's sack (Gen 44:2). After the brothers had gone a little way, Joseph sent his steward after the brothers to accuse them of stealing the cup. They denied it and even offered the life of the one who was found with it (not imagining that it was in any of their sacks) (Gen 44:9). It was found in Benjamin's sack, and the brothers were taken before Joseph, who said he was going to make Benjamin a slave for what "he" had done (Gen 44:17).

This is the peak of the story, and what happens next is very important. It would be within character for the brothers to just say, "Okay, see ya later, Ben." Instead, Judah offered his life in place of Benjamin's (Gen 44:33). (Again, remember, slavery is a picture of death in this story.) Judah is a type of Christ in this story, offering his life in place of another. Judah, the one who married a Canaanite and slept with a shrine prostitute, now showed the deepest kind of love for his brother and father. This is truly a transformation from the brothers' treatment of Joseph earlier in the narrative.

Judah's sacrificial love in this part of the story helps us understand why God chose Judah to continue the Messianic seed-line. Judah had proven himself to be the "king" among his brothers. A king's job is to be the representative head of his people, and part of that job is dying for your people. Judah offered his life as a king in place of Benjamin's. While Joseph is a picture of Christ, Judah is a better picture of Christ. Joseph did not willingly go into slavery, but Judah willingly offered to die for his brother to honor his father.

At this point, Joseph revealed himself to his brothers, and they had a tearful reunion (Gen 45:1-14). Pharaoh's house was full of joy on account of this restoration (Gen 45:16). (They were apparently Yahweh worshipers too, indicating that Joseph had been sharing the gospel with them.) The restoration was full and joyous and complete, and Joseph invited his brothers and father to move to the finest land in Egypt.

When the brothers returned to Canaan to tell Jacob what had happened, he at first wouldn't believe them, and "his heart turned cold" (Gen 45:26*), which is a type of death. Then he saw how much they had been blessed by the Egyptians and his "spirit...revived" (Gen 45:27), which

Unit 4: Jacob's Family

is a type of resurrection. And the whole family made plans to move to Egypt.

This lesson provides a very helpful approach to understanding how transformation works. When the brothers first came to Egypt, we have no indication that they had reformed from how they had treated Joseph. For all we know, they would have been content to leave Simeon to rot in prison in Egypt like they had done to Joseph. Notice how God and Joseph (or God through Joseph) brought about their transformation.

First, God made sure that the famine continued so that the brothers had to go back to Egypt to rescue Simeon. God often uses the circumstances in our lives to direct us toward maturity. Second, because of Joseph's demand for them to bring Benjamin back, they were forced to face the seriousness of their sin against their father when they sold Joseph; Jacob had experienced the loss of Joseph as a sort of death. Finally, when Joseph "framed" Benjamin, the brothers were forced to face the cruelty of what they had done to Joseph the first time and consider how it would affect their father. When God tests us, the tests don't just *reveal* who we are, they *change* who we are. Judah went from being the brother who was leading the charge to sell Joseph into slavery to being the brother who offered his life as a slave in place of Benjamin's. God's tests are redemptive.

APPLICATION

The story of the redemption of Joseph's brothers teaches us about how God works to change us. He arranges the circumstances and the people in our lives to lead us into tests that transform us. Psalm 11 praises God because He tests the righteous. Proverbs 3:5-6 tells us to trust in God because He is guiding our paths.

Are you presently going through any transformative tests at the hands of the Lord? Are there any trials, acts of divine discipline, or simply difficult circumstances or relationships in your life? Those aren't random—God gives us just what He needs for us to have in our lives in order to grow. Identify areas where you need to change; put these changes into practice, and see what God does in your heart as a result.

ACTIVITIES

2. Journal Time. Reflect on how God has transformed your life and answer the questions below.

Reflect on your life; do you see any circumstances in your past that God has used to transform you? What were they?_____

_____

_____

_____

Lesson 4.4

How did you respond in these circumstances? What, if anything, would you do differently now?
_____
_____
_____

Are there any situations in your life currently that God is using to test and transform you? If you can't think of any, ask God to reveal them to you. Think of any challenging things in your life and ask God what He wants to teach you through these situations. _____
_____
_____
_____

EVALUATION

1. How do we know that Joseph had already forgiven his brothers? _____
_____
_____

2. If this story isn't about Joseph forgiving his brothers, what is it about? _____
_____
_____
_____

3. What were the three tests that Joseph led his brothers through? _____
_____
_____
_____

4. Who showed the greatest compassion toward his father and Benjamin in the story and what did he do? _____
_____
_____

LESSON 4.5

Joseph Restored to His Family

UNIT 4

THE STORY

Lesson Theme - The hope that Jacob's family would return to the promised land

This lesson is about *hope*. The nation of Israel moved to the land of Egypt *even though* Canaan was the promised land. God spoke to Jacob in a vision and assured him that it was okay to go to Egypt for He would make them into a nation there and bring them back to Canaan (Gen 46:2-4). The rest of the story bears out Jacob's (and Joseph's) firm conviction that this return to the promised land would indeed happen. God's promise to Abraham, Isaac and Jacob would surely be fulfilled, but the nation of Israel would come of age in exile. Like Joseph, they would suffer in a foreign land before they inherited the promised land.

Up to this point in the story, Jacob's family was just that: a family—brothers, a sister, father and mothers. Note also that they were a relatively small family (only 70 people in all—Gen 46:27) and were not wealthy anymore, for the famine had wiped out most of Jacob's wealth. They would be a nation per the promises to Abraham, Isaac and Jacob, but not yet. Several of the last lessons have been coming of age stories—of Jacob, Joseph and Judah. Here we see the beginning of the coming of age story of the nation of Israel. And the nation came of age away from home, in exile. So Jacob and his family went to Egypt to *become* a nation.

Judah is a good example of what would happen if the nation of Israel came of age in Canaan. They would intermarry with the Canaanites, sleep with their prostitutes and worship their gods. Egypt didn't present the same temptation as the land of Canaan did since Egyptians despised shepherds like Jacob and his family (Gen 46:34). Coming of age in Egypt was a blessing for Israel; it was a protection from Canaanite contamination. Furthermore, the timing for Israel to claim Canaan was not yet right. Noah had pronounced a curse on the Canaanites, but God had told Abram that his descendants wouldn't claim the land yet since "the iniquity of the Amorites [was]

OVERVIEW

In response to the news that Joseph was still alive and God's prompting him to move to Egypt, Jacob packed up his things and family and *left* the promised land to move to Goshen in Egypt. He believed that God would raise the nation there and bring them back home. His hope was firm. Jacob grew old in Egypt and blessed his sons there with the hope of return. Judah received the blessing of rulership, and Joseph received the double inheritance of the firstborn; the other sons each received a prophetic blessing. Jacob and Joseph both died in Egypt and told their family to bury them back in Canaan because of their firm hope in God's promises.

SOURCE MATERIAL

- Genesis 46-50
- Psalm 137
- Proverbs 10:1

Unit 4: Jacob's Family

OBJECTIVES

Feel...

- gratitude for the restoration of Jacob and Joseph.
- gratitude for God's provision for Jacob's family.
- a sense of hope for the return of Israel to the promised land.
- a feeling of exile for yourself as you "come of age" in a foreign land rather than in the kingdom of God.

Understand...

- that it was God's will for the nation of Israel to "come of age" in Egypt.
- that Joseph, Jacob and the rest of them were firmly convinced of God's faithfulness and their hope of returning to the promised land.
- that Joseph and Judah both ended up with a piece of the covenantal blessing.
- that Jacob and Joseph both wanted to be buried back in the promised land.
- that as Christians, we are "coming of age" in a foreign land which demands a certain kind of behavior and faith.

Apply this understanding by...

- determining areas of exile in your life.
- considering how you have behaved in the past in these areas of exile and how you should behave in the future.

not yet complete" (Gen 15:16). Israel, God told Abram, would serve another nation who would afflict them for 400 years.

In Genesis 47:13-26 we get some details about how Joseph dealt with the famine as it worsened in Egypt. In order to feed the Egyptians, Joseph first sold them grain in exchange for all their silver and livestock; finally, he bought up all of their land as well. Joseph had proven himself to be a shrewd ruler, and so our expectation at this point in the story is that he would be the one to receive the rulership blessing from Jacob. We will see that this would not be the case. However, while Joseph was shrewd, not everything he did was great. He set the stage for great abuse by the Egyptian government later on; they even enslaved the Israelites to provide labor for the projects they were working on. Joseph and Pharaoh treated the Israelites well at this point, but future Pharaohs would not.

As we have seen in previous lessons, blessings from patriarchs in the seed-line have incredible power. Noah's blessing upon Canaan and Shem was already coming to pass. Likewise, Jacob's blessing on his sons amounted to nothing less than prophecy. These sons *would* become what Jacob spoke in his blessings. Jacob's blessings on his sons revealed his *hope* for the future. There was no doubt in Jacob's mind that the nation would return to the land of Canaan and possess it.

One of the ongoing questions in the Jacob narrative has been: would Judah or Joseph get the covenantal blessing of the firstborn? We already know that Rueben, Simeon and Levi had forfeited that blessing by their behavior. Judah was most likely the fourth (of Rachel and Leah's sons) and therefore would be next in line. Joseph, however, had proven himself to be faithful and a good ruler, while Judah made some really bad decisions in Canaan. The blessing ends up being somewhat split between them. Normally, the firstborn would get a double portion of the inheritance and the blessing of being a ruler. Here, however, Joseph received the double portion, and Judah got the blessing of rulership. Even though Joseph had proven himself to be a shrewd ruler, Judah had proven that he was willing to sacrifice himself for the youngest son; and sacrifice is the ultimate kingly act. Joseph received a double inheritance; his first two sons were reckoned among Jacob's sons. Therefore, Joseph, through his sons, would receive double the inheritance when they came into the land.

Judah's blessing recorded in Genesis 49:8-12 is another early prophecy of the coming Messiah. First, there is a prophecy that Judah's hand will be on the neck of his enemies. Judah was the next in the seed-line, and this prophecy is a continuation of the promise that a seed of the woman would crush the head of the serpent. Additionally, there is a promise that the scepter of ruling authority would not depart from Judah; so we see that the Messiah would not only be a head-crusher, but also a king. Finally, there are some prophecies reminding us of specific things that Jesus did: riding on a donkey's colt and having His clothes covered in the "blood of grapes" (Gen 49:11)—an allusion to Jesus' death, to the bloody defeat of His enemies, and to the wine of communion.

This lesson ends with the stories of Jacob and Joseph's deaths, reminding us of the theme of hope. Both Jacob and Joseph believed that the nation would return to Canaan. Jacob insisted on being buried there while his sons were still alive (Gen 49:29-33), and Joseph told his family to bring his body back and bury him there when they returned to Canaan as a nation (Gen 50:24-25). Their hope was not in this life, but it was on this earth.

APPLICATION

The point of application is that we too are "In exile," coming of age in a foreign land, but we have *hope*. We sojourn in a land where Jesus is not called King; we live among people who don't know the God who created them; we are surrounded by all forms of immorality, wickedness, greed and idolatry; and it is in this place that God is calling us into maturity. We are coming of age in a foreign land, but we have hope. So what do we do? What is our job here? To carve out little pieces of land in this world, put a stake in the ground and claim it for Jesus Christ. Not because we don't have a kingdom, but because we know that we *do* have a kingdom, just not here, not yet. If you are a member of a family who believes Jesus is Lord, then your house is part of that kingdom; your church is part of that kingdom as well.

In all likelihood, we will, like Jacob and Joseph, die here, in the land of our exile. That's okay; we will return. Jesus is going to come back, and His kingdom will be without end; the scepter of Judah will not depart from His hand. And each of us will be raised from the dead, and all of this land will be claimed for the glory of the Father under the authority of His son.

For now, how you act in sojourn will determine how prepared you are when you come into the kingdom. Are you like Judah, quick to repent when confronted with your sins and willing to sacrifice for your brothers? Are you like Joseph, faithful and honest even when suffering in a foreign land? Do you *believe* in the hope that you profess?

Unit 4: Jacob's Family

ACTIVITIES

1. Personal Reflection: Our Land of Exile. The land of Canaan was home for Jacob's family, and God had them move to a foreign land. Still, Jacob's family was called to hope in the coming of their return to the land. We too are in a foreign land. In the space below, draw all of the places you spend most of your time: home, school, church, your friend's house and your favorite hangout (any other relevant places too). Circle the picture that shows where you feel the most "at home" and write a sentence explaining why you feel more at home there than in any of the other places.

2. Messianic Prophecy. Read Judah's blessing in Genesis 49:8-12. Then write down how Jesus fulfilled the prophecies in this blessing. _____

_____

_____

_____

_____

_____

_____

Lesson 4.5

EVALUATION

1. How did Jacob know that it was okay to move his family to Egypt? _____
_____
_____

2. Who received the covenantal blessing of the firstborn? _____
_____
_____

3. Follow-up: why did these two each receive firstborn blessings and the others didn't? _____
_____
_____
_____

4. Who continued the head-crushing seed-line? _____

5. Why did Joseph and Jacob both want to be buried in Canaan? _____
_____
_____

www.ingramcontent.com/pod-product-compliance
Lightning Source LLC
Chambersburg PA
CBHW081338080526
44588CB00017B/2663